Detroit Speed's

How to Build a

PRO TOURING CAR

Tommy Lee Byrd and Kyle Tucker

S-A DESIGN

CarTech®

CarTech®

CarTech®, Inc.
39966 Grand Avenue
North Branch, MN 55056
Phone: 651-277-1200 or 800-551-4754
Fax: 651-277-1203
www.cartechbooks.com

Edit by Bob Wilson and Wes Eisenschenk
Layout by Monica Seiberlich

ISBN 978-1-61325-137-9
Item No. SA293

Library of Congress Cataloging-in-Publication Data

Byrd, Tommy Lee
 Detroit Speed's how to build a pro touring car / by Tommy Lee Byrd and Kyle Tucker.
    pages cm
 ISBN 978-1-61325-137-9
1. Hot rods. 2. Muscle cars–Customizing. 3. Antique and classic automobiles–Customizing. 4. Muscle cars–Performance. 5. Automobiles, Home-built. I. Tucker, Kyle, author. II. Title. III. Title: How to build a Pro Touring car.

 TL236.3.B967 2014
 629.228›6–dc23

 2014006978

Written, edited, and designed in the U.S.A.
Printed in China
10 9 8 7 6 5 4 3 2 1

Title Page:
Pro Touring cars almost always have a hunkered-down stance to lower the car's center of gravity, thus decreasing the likelihood of body roll. This 1967 Corvette offers a perfect blend of classic style and modern performance, thanks to a late-model suspension, large Baer brakes, and LS7 power plant.

Back Cover Photos

Top Left:
This is a 1968 Camaro with stock tubs. The rear tires are 235/45R17s, mounted to 17 x 8–inch wheels. It offers a great look for a mild-mannered Pro Touring build, but most folks want a much wider-tire and-wheel combination out back.

Top Right:
Air tools can be used to speed up this installation but it's much more precise to do the work by hand. It's easier to notice issues, such as binding, when installing nuts and bolts with simple hand tools. After the installation is complete and the car is at ride height, torque the control arm bolts to 120 ft-lbs.

Bottom Left:
When the car reached completion, the Detroit Speed crew lowered the 1969 Camaro body over the new subframe and bolted it into place. Other modifications had already been performed, so this was one of the final steps to getting the car back on its feet.

Bottom Right:
Bolt the one-piece aluminum bracket to the axle flange using four Grade-8 bolts and nuts. This backing plate serves as the caliper mount. It also holds the internal parking brake assembly, which is essentially a drum brake inside the hat.

OVERSEAS DISTRIBUTION BY:

PGUK
63 Hatton Garden
London EC1N 8LE, England
Phone: 020 7061 1980 • Fax: 020 7242 3725
www.pguk.co.uk

Renniks Publications Ltd.
3/37-39 Green Street
Banksmeadow, NSW 2109, Australia
Phone: 2 9695 7055 • Fax: 2 9695 7355
www.renniks.com

CONTENTS

FOREWORD by Kyle Busch

As a NASCAR driver, touring the country, I spend my fair share of time behind the wheel, and it's where I feel at home. I've always been a fan of all kinds of cars. I love muscle cars, old hot rods, and luxury cars.

Whether it's on the racetrack or out on the open road, I demand a lot from any car that I'm driving. Many of the same characteristics that I challenge my crew chiefs to provide are what I was looking for when I took my 1969 Camaro to Detroit Speed for a Pro Touring makeover. I wanted them to turn a car that was an old beater into a car that drives, rides, accelerates, shifts, and stops better than any other car I had ever driven. I knew this would be a tough task and never dreamed that they could take a car built in 1969 and turn it into something that outperforms vehicles of the modern era.

The first time I drove my original 1969 Camaro, it wasn't a pleasant experience, and even for a professional race car driver it was a rough adjustment. The car drove like a boat—the front and rear floated up and down, and I was never sure which way it was going to go next. The thing bounced from one side of the road to the other, and with an old worn-out steering box, I struggled just trying to keep it in my own lane. With a not-so-smooth-shifting transmission that felt like it had 24 inches of shifter throw, I definitely would never be able to beat another competitor down the strip. With all the up-and-down and side-to-side

motion, you'd hope that the thing would at least have good stopping power, but I could write this whole foreword before I got it to stop, especially when slowing down from highway speeds.

Enter Detroit Speed and the Pro Touring package that turned my Camaro from an old boat into my dream yacht. My list of demands where high: I wanted to go all out with this car and turn it into something I would never want to get rid of. I wanted something that looked cool and drove like a dream, and that's exactly what I ended up with. After watching this build happen at Detroit speed in Mooresville, close to my KBM shop, I couldn't wait to get behind the wheel and drive!

First, it looked amazing! I love the paint colors and all the accents that make this car mine. It truly is a work of art.

Next, the sound. We fired it up and it came to life with a punch. It got my heart racing with how loud it was and how smooth it rumbled at idle.

Sitting in it and feeling the sunken seats with leather wrapped around you, the four-point belts holding you in tight, the gauges in your face, and the pedals at your feet is an experience that mixes the practical and safe features of my race cars with the comfort of a high-end sports car.

Finally, the drive. I grabbed first gear and let out the clutch to some-

thing much better than I could have ever imagined. It was awesome to feel it roll. As I turned the steering wheel with the new rack-and-pinion steering, it was responsive and ate up the road as I drove the car away. It felt great.

Then I had to check out how well it stopped. Wow! On a dime. Again, it actually was better than I expected. It didn't take a ton of pressure or have a ton of pedal travel to make it stop.

It was nothing like what it was before. The engine sounds great, acceleration feels great, brakes are awesome. The car had a sports car feel in the suspension that allowed you to have a ton of confidence in driving it in your own lane and going where you wanted to go, *not where it wanted to go*. It is a smooth and comfortable ride, while also being able to corner hard and keep all four tires under you. It always teases you to drive it harder.

I can't thank everyone at Detroit Speed enough for the job they did with putting the Pro Touring treatment on my 1969 Camaro. The thing is a blast to drive and something that I will never part with.

Because the first-generation Camaro is still the most popular choice for a Pro Touring build, this book provides step-by-step instructions for taking a stock 1969 Camaro and making it handle and perform better than a new sports car. The buildup features the most generic platform and provides outstanding results when complete.

These steps can be used for other builds also, as most muscle cars feature a coil-spring independent front suspension and a solid rear axle, with either a leaf-spring or multi-link coil-spring rear suspension. This buildup also includes braking systems, tires and wheels, engine upgrades, and much more, in an effort to squeeze every ounce of performance out of a classic Camaro.

Chapter 1 gives you an overview of Pro Touring by answering these questions: What does Pro Touring have to offer you? Which makes and models are best suited for Pro Touring? Who is Detroit Speed?

Chapter 2 discusses the skills you need to accomplish a successful Pro Touring build and where is best to take on the project. Also, a fairly complete list of needed tools is provided.

Other important factors in a Pro Touring build involve the chassis structure: whether your car rides on a full frame or features a unibody construction. Many modifications provide rigidity to the chassis, which helps high-performance suspension components do their jobs efficiently.

If the chassis isn't strong enough to handle the abuse, the best parts in the world do not provide the ideal result. Braces and other support brackets are a great addition to any full-frame car, although subframe connectors are a must-have for anyone using a unibody vehicle, such as a Camaro, Mustang, or any of the popular mid-size Mopars. Chassis and structural bracing are covered in Chapter 3.

All front suspension styles and components are discussed in Chapter 4. Chapter 5 covers everything for the rear suspension.

Chapters 6 and 7 reveal the ins and outs of the most desirable braking systems, as well as tire and wheel combinations that provide good looks and awesome performance. In Chapter 7 you also learn what it takes to fit the largest possible tires and wheels on your Pro Touring build.

Of all the traits of a Pro Touring car, the one that appeals to all car guys is horsepower, and that is the focus of Chapter 8. Any custom build, whether it's geared toward drag racing, road racing, or anything in between, needs horsepower to complete the gearhead experience. Although horsepower is always a popular bragging point for any build, the way horsepower is made has changed drastically in the past 15 years or so.

With the development of the LS family of engines, as well as the popular overhead cam engines from the Ford camp and the new Hemi from Mopar, it's very popular to swap a late-model engine into a vintage body. With a plethora of products, including headers, wiring harnesses, and engine mounting kits, it's even easier to bring your muscle car out of the Stone Age, compared to the experimental engine swaps of years past.

You can make big power with modern engines without spending crazy amounts of money on race-only

Throughout this book, you see the necessary steps to turn a stock Camaro into a full-on Pro Touring machine. Some folks start with a complete driver, whereas others pick up a project that someone else gave up on. Regardless, the process is the same and the end result is definitely worth the effort.

Chapter 4 covers front suspension and Kyle Tucker provides insight into the advantages of Detroit Speed components. His extensive knowledge in product development and real-world muscle car performance have earned him respect in the aftermarket industry.

Rear suspension is covered in Chapter 5, where you follow along with the installation of Detroit Speed's QUADRALink rear suspension system. It replaces the original leaf springs and provides a killer suspension that really works.

Old-school big-blocks are still a great option for many muscle car applications but the real problem with these engines is weight. For a Pro Touring build, you're looking for a nearly perfect weight balance from front to rear, and a big-block puts an extra couple hundred pounds on the nose.

parts. They're dependable, powerful, and surprisingly fuel-efficient. It's not uncommon for a 500-hp V-8 engine to get fuel mileage in the mid-20 range, something that was unheard of in the muscle car era. Although big-blocks ruled when gas was cheap, they just don't stack up to the new wave of power plants from the Big Three manufacturers.

What's the biggest disadvantage? This can be answered with one word:

weight. Big-blocks, and old-school small-blocks for that matter, are heavy beasts. The weight differences of various engine combinations are covered more thoroughly in Chapter 8, and you quickly appreciate the reason most folks opt for a modern engine in a Pro Touring car.

In Chapter 9 you find a complete guide to wiring and plumbing your car, including some fuel system tricks and tips.

Chapter 10 showcases some great examples of real-world Pro Touring cars, including a 1969 Camaro, 1966 Mustang, 1963 Chevy II, and 1965 Chevelle.

Engine swaps are very popular in the Pro Touring movement. For most GM vehicles, the go-to platform is the LS family of engines. These engines are surprisingly affordable and make incredible horsepower. This particular engine is an all-aluminum LS6, topped with a Magnuson supercharger, making nearly 600 hp.

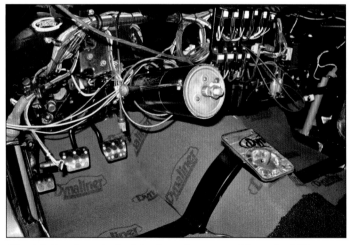

Most folks dread electrical work on an old car but it's essential to the reliability of a Pro Touring car. You learn everything you need to know about wiring and plumbing in Chapter 9 as you follow along with the 1969 Camaro project car.

PRO TOURING EXPLAINED

If you're reading this book, chances are that you want to build a Pro Touring car, or at least learn more about them. The term *Pro Touring* describes more than just a simple trend in the car hobby; it describes cars that are purpose-built for performance, while retaining the classic looks of a muscle car. Pro Touring cars generally do not see an easy life, even though the build quality is superb in most cases. The point is to create a car that accelerates, corners, and stops better than a new performance car, without tarnishing the body styles that we all know and love.

To build a Pro Touring car, you must first know what the term entails. It's more than just slapping a set of large-diameter wheels on an old car and lowering the ride height. If it were that easy, you wouldn't need to read a book to figure out all of the tricks to make it happen. A textbook Pro Touring car has custom front and rear suspension, as well as highly upgraded braking components, wide tires on all four corners, and lots of parts that help stiffen the chassis structure. All components play an important role in building a successful Pro Touring car; this book explains the details of each series of modifications and the results that follow.

Through the years of automotive customizing, many trends have come and gone. There was a time when muscle car enthusiasts put a set of N50-15 tires on the back of their car, bolted on a set of traction bars, and installed headers to create a custom car. It really didn't take much thought to create a cool car, because of the lack of custom components in the automotive aftermarket.

The progression of modifications made for some interesting creations in the 1970s and early 1980s, but a new idea in the late 1980s turned the automotive aftermarket on its ear. They didn't know what to call it but the idea involved a 1969 Camaro body and a full-on road race chassis. *Big Red* was its name, and it was unlike anything that had ever been built. The goal was to run 200 mph

The mark of a good Pro Touring build is the ability to get in, fire it up, and hit the road. Generally, no extraordinary maintenance is needed, and you can enjoy the advantages of modern fuel injection, high-tech suspension, and super-wide tires.

Pro Touring cars almost always have a hunkered-down stance to lower the car's center of gravity, thus decreasing the likelihood of body roll. This 1967 Corvette offers a perfect blend of classic style and modern performance, thanks to a late-model suspension, large Baer brakes, and LS7 power plant.

In addition to suspension modifications, most Pro Touring cars have large disc brakes on all four corners and large-diameter (usually 17-inch or larger) wheels. Wheel widths vary from 8 inches all the way up to 12 inches, depending mostly on the car's wheel tub and frame rail configuration.

but make the body look as stock as possible. Dan and R. J. Gottlieb built the car, and the result sparked the Pro Touring movement.

Although *Big Red* had a huge influence on the Pro Touring movement, Mark Stielow really got it started, and did so in a car that was a little more street-friendly. You'll see his name a few more times in this book, as he is still a strong force in the Pro Touring scene.

The early Pro Touring cars featured wide tires on all four corners and a hunkered-down stance that received lots of attention from the media, since it was a fresh, new take

on a beloved body style. The automotive world had not seen this big a breakthrough since the first Pro Street car rolled out of Scott Sullivan's shop in 1979. That particular Pro Street car took modifications that were seen only on the drag strip and blended them with a 1967 Chevy II street car. The Pro Touring style took this same blending approach, except that the object was to carve corners instead of straight-line performance.

As for the name *Pro Touring*, it was a term that Mark Stielow and longtime magazine editor Jeff Smith coined in the April 1998 issue of *Chevy High Performance*. Mark's inten-

tion with the Pro Touring name was to refer to European touring cars and the handling capabilities that went along with them. *Touring* also referred to events such as the Hot Rod Power Tour, which required these modified muscle cars to run for long distances without the need for constant repairs. Mark mentioned the term, Jeff used it frequently in his magazine efforts, and the rest is history!

Although a certain few cars kicked off the idea, it took quite a few years for the automotive aftermarket to catch on and start manufacturing products that made it easy for folks to turn a standard muscle car into a high-performance machine. The company that set the standard for high-quality go-fast parts is Detroit Speed (this book follows along with a complete build to show you how to build your very own Pro Touring car).

Detroit Speed builds products that are track-tested for performance and street-tested for durability, which makes the company a standout in a sea of competing manufacturers. Many of its products are bolt-in replacements for factory components, making it easy to convert your sloppy muscle car suspension into a masterpiece of precisely engineered products that really work!

Why Pro Touring?

If you've ever driven a stock or modified muscle car, you know they are usually a headache to drive. It's all part of the experience of driving an old car but it certainly has its downsides when you're sitting in traffic or perhaps carving through a mountain road. Lots of them came with manual brakes, manual steering, and temperamental transmissions that only get worse with age. They are a

George Poteet's Talladega-inspired 1969 Ford Torino was built by Troy Trepanier and is one of the most detailed Pro Touring builds of all time. With that said, it isn't exactly practical because of the extreme show car quality, and it certainly isn't attainable by the average enthusiast.

This is what the average enthusiast can expect to find in his or her own garage: a first-generation Camaro scattered into a million pieces. Luckily, parts are affordable, and any gearhead with the appropriate tools can do the necessary work to make it a killer Pro Touring car.

Bone-stock muscle cars have lots of cool factor but it's rather disappointing when you expect it to handle well. Soft suspension, sloppy steering, and small brakes are the biggest obstacles to tackle. You can see this Camaro is not quite ready to hit the autocross course with its old-school Firestone Wide Oval tires.

bear to drive in stock form, and those characteristics are even worse when straight-line performance is the goal. Street/strip and drag cars are usually miserably loud and uncomfortable to drive. They're super cool and serve a great purpose but if you want a car that you can really enjoy, a Pro Touring build makes the most sense.

In the grand scheme of things, you have a lot of choices when it comes to building a muscle car. Some folks like to keep things original and brag about matching numbers, low mileage, and the car's maintenance records. If that's what you're into, mini-tubs, big tires, and a lowered stance may not be the answer, but that one is pretty obvious.

Drag racing guys are obviously on the other side of the fence. It's sometimes confusing with the Pro Touring look-alikes, however. These

Street/strip cars are multi-purpose builds but they don't share the practicality of a Pro Touring build. This 1967 Chevelle is wickedly fast, yet tame on the street; still, at the end of the day, it just isn't as easy to drive as a similarly prepared Pro Touring car.

This 1968 Pontiac Firebird is a prime example of a simple and practical Pro Touring build with its lowered ride height, Baer disc brakes, and wide rubber on all four corners. Firebirds and Trans Ams make for great Pro Touring cars because they're distinct and the parts interchange with Camaro platforms making for an easy build.

Stock muscle cars are fairly decent when it comes to straight-line performance, but as soon as you throw them into the curves, this is the result. Body roll is the enemy with a Pro Touring build. To combat it you want to stiffen the suspension and help the camber stay more consistent through the suspension cycle.

mimic the Pro Touring look with a lower ride height and large-diameter wheels. The reality of most of these builds is that the owners simply cut the coil springs up front and install lowering blocks in the rear to achieve the right stance. This does very little to help the handling of a car but it's certainly the cheapest way to give your car the Pro Touring look. Although this is a perfectly common practice, it's not exactly what Pro Touring is about.

Performance

A fact that most of us want to deny is that our favorite muscle cars are quite lazy when it comes to realistic performance. Yes, it might make more than 400 hp and, yes, it might run 12s in the quarter-mile, but when you line up a stock 1969 Camaro SS against a stock Mazda Miata on an autocross course, you will likely be embarrassed. The idea of a Pro Touring build is to reduce body roll, increase traction, and reduce weight (or at least shift it around to help balance the car). The further you dip into each of those three traits, the better your car performs.

Reducing body roll helps plant all four tires evenly. Increasing traction means you can hit the corners harder and faster. Reducing weight means that your muscle car uses its horsepower more efficiently, and the weight balance greatly affects the car's traction and handling.

Another important aspect of any Pro Touring build is the braking system. You can have thousands of dollars' worth of suspension underneath your vehicle but if the brakes aren't up

Although appearance is part of the equation, performance is one of the highly acclaimed characteristics of building a Pro Touring car. Kyle Tucker wheels the Detroit Speed second-generation test car through the autocross course at LS Fest in Bowling Green, Kentucky. This car is at the top of the food chain when it comes to Pro Touring.

The idea of a Pro Touring build is to blend the looks of a vintage muscle car with the new technologies of today's performance cars. You can create a great-looking machine in the process. This 1969 Mustang is a great example. Its low stance and wheel combination provide a look that seems very natural for the car.

to the task, your lap times and overall driving experience suffers. Stopping power is worth every penny, and can make a 3,400-pound Camaro feel like a high-end sports car.

Appearance

Although the performance function of a Pro Touring car is generally the main focus, the end result is almost always a muscle car with an aggressive race-ready look that everyone loves. In this case, all of the aspects that make the car perform well also provide a great overall appearance. Detroit Speed perfected the balance of good looks and incredible performance, and the company continues to crank out products that help your muscle car look good and go fast.

Practicality

The balance of performance and practicality in the Pro Touring following is certainly noteworthy. It's easy to be carried away, so if money is no object, you could put a 1969 Camaro skin on top of a NASCAR chassis and have the wildest setup on the block. But then you're looking at the inconvenience of using racing slicks and exotic fuels, and trailering the car to each destination. Let's face it: that becomes more work and less fun. That's where balance comes in, and Detroit Speed nails it in every new line of products with components that combine race-inspired development with street-friendly driving characteristics. When you're behind the wheel of a Pro Touring car, the drive should be comfortable but have the capability of handling harsh cornering, heavy braking, and wide-open acceleration without the limitations of sloppy stock components.

As with any custom build, it's easy to get carried away and end up with a full-on race car. Ken Thompson, from Mooresville, North Carolina, built this incredible Ford Falcon using every ounce of his outstanding fabrication skills. Although impressive, let's file this one away as overkill for the average Pro Touring enthusiast.

Even though it's over the top in terms of the average guy's budget and skill set, Ken Thompson's Falcon deserves a closer look. The car features a NASCAR-style chassis and suspension, along with this awesome 278-ci Ford Indy Car engine, fit with a single turbocharger. It makes crazy horsepower and handles anything Ken can throw at it.

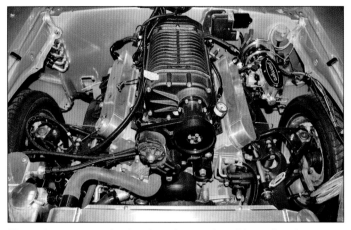

If you have a car that's already running, it's a simple weekend project to update the front suspension, thanks to products from Detroit Speed. New tubular control arms, coil-overs, spindles, and sway bars are easy installs that might prevent you from doing a complete teardown.

The joy of building a Pro Touring car is seeing the results of your modifications. Every one makes a difference in the way the car feels and performs. Every component has a job, and it's Detroit Speed's goal to make them strong, efficient, and reliable.

Building a Pro Touring car is not as easy as it sounds, but with the right components you can transform a sluggish muscle car into a machine that reacts quickly, does what you tell it to do, and takes you to work a few times a week if you want it to. Practical performance with classic muscle car style. Does it get any better than that?

The early days of Pro Touring were all about innovation but today's market is much easier to get into for the average car guy. Complete suspension packages are available, and they are certainly the suggested approach; nonetheless, it's easy to pick individual components if you'd rather take it slow with your project. Going piece by piece allows you to ease into the Pro Touring realm, without spending a big chunk of money from the get-go.

Some folks start the process with a bigger sway bar, upgraded shocks, and good brakes, but at the end of the day, most end up with the same components that are in a complete kit. You have two options: spend $1,000 at a time and slowly work your way into a car that handles well, or lay down all the cash at once and transform your lazy muscle car into a corner-carving machine in one fell swoop.

Choose Your Poison

Let's face it, any sort of custom car build is going to cost money, and it is something that swirls around your brain until the moment it is finished. Ideas flow in and out, budgets fluctuate, and distractions get in the way but you will likely be addicted to thinking, building, and buying parts for your Pro Touring car. With all of this in mind, what type of car do you want to build?

Pro Touring builds generally consist of a car from the muscle car era, meaning a midsize car built between 1964 and 1972. This isn't always the

Some folks like the midsize classics from the 1960s and 1970s, such as GM's A-Body platform that rode beneath the Chevrolet Chevelle, Buick Skylark (GS), Oldsmobile Cutlass (442), and Pontiac Tempest (GTO). This bright red 1966 Chevelle is owned by Bob Bowe and offers a great mix of practicality and performance.

Although most of this book focuses on GM F-Body plat-forms, the Nova crowd needs to listen closely because nearly all early F-Body suspension components inter-change with the 1968–1972 X-Body platform. This opens the door for all sorts of cool builds, including this all-out Pro Touring machine owned by Mark Turner.

The GM F-Body platform is so popular and widely avail-able that it makes a lot of sense to build a first- or second-generation Camaro. The product support is out-standing, and you can ease your way into it with a simple set of springs and sway bars, or go all out with a custom Detroit Speed subframe kit.

case, as some owners like to step out-side the box in an effort to create a wild combination from an unlikely source. Sometimes it comes down to a lifelong desire to own a partic-ular car; perhaps, it's a car that you owned in high school, or a car that your father or other family mem-ber owned, or simply something you've always wanted. Everyone has different tastes, so the Pro Touring movement is full of diverse combi-nations, built from a wide variety of platforms. GM vehicles certainly win the battle of most popular in the Pro Touring hobby because of parts availability and the fact that General Motors made a bunch of really cool cars during the muscle car era.

GM Cars

Camaros are undoubtedly the most popular platform in the Pro Touring hobby because they are easily attainable, they have tons of aftermar-ket product support, and they're just plain cool. First-generation Camaros (1967–1969) and third-generation Novas (1968–1974) share very similar suspension designs, so the immense

popularity of the Camaro naturally trickles down to the Nova, because of the parts interchange. Before 1968, the Nova (commonly known as the Chevy II) featured a totally different platform, and the cars were much smaller.

From 1962 to 1967, Chevy IIs were affordable compact cars, with an optional V-8 engine beginning in 1964, making these lightweight cars very popular with folks who like to go fast. The 1962–1967 Chevy II market is hotter than ever, and you can still pick one up at a reasonable

price and expect the same great prod-uct support as with the later-model Nova platform.

It's easy to have tunnel vision when dealing with Pro Touring builds because you see so many midsize GM cars in the show field. Camaros, Novas, and Chevelles are quite common but don't be discour-aged if you prefer another brand or even some peculiar designs. There is almost always a way to make an old car handle like a new one. Some peo-ple like to give full-size cars, includ-ing station wagons, the Pro Touring

It doesn't always have to be about Camaros, Novas, and Chevelles if you're a Chevrolet junkie. This 1970 Impala certainly gets a lot of looks with its low-down stance and large-diameter tire and wheel combination. It's tough to make a big, heavy car handle well but it's not impossible!

Ford platforms are a bit tricky because of the front suspension design, which involves mounting the spring and shock assembly on top of the upper control arm. This configuration does not have good geometry, and the bulky shock towers create a cramped engine bay. Ford guys generally have to get creative when it comes to getting the stance just right, but this Bobby Alloway–built Fairlane sits very low.

Ford Mustangs are a little easier to tackle, as a number of manufacturers, including Detroit Speed, offer suspension packages for most 1964–1970 Mustangs. By altering the suspension geometry, and reducing body roll, these cars can really handle well. Add a set of big brakes and sticky tires and you have a serious Pro Touring car.

look and feel, which is perfectly cool in the eyes of any car guy. Who wouldn't love to see a big, heavy car out there holding its own in a sea of Camaros?

Ford Cars

Ford offered a number of great choices for performance in the 1960s and 1970s, so if you're a lover of the Blue Oval, you have plenty of options. Mustang is the prime choice, thanks to its lightweight unibody construction, good weight distribution, and vast aftermarket product support. You can also consider a compact cruiser, such as a Ford Falcon, step up to the midsize Fairlane, or go large with the Galaxie.

High-tech Pro Touring parts are not always available for every make and model but you'd be surprised at the product innovations in the past decade. Ford folks don't quite have it as easy as the GM crowd when it comes to easy suspension swaps and parts availability but it won't take long to catch up. In fact, Detroit Speed recently introduced its

line of Mustang Aluma-Frame and QUADRALink suspension systems to fit 1964½–1970 Mustangs. Find out more on page 49.

Mopar Cars

What about the Mopar guys? You know there are lots of them out there, so why are there so few Mopars in the Pro Touring world? It all comes down to a suspension design that isn't conducive to road racing or autocross racing. Lots of Mopar muscle cars had torsion-bar front suspension and leaf-spring rear suspension; it's a suitable design for some forms of racing but it just doesn't provide the same

advantages as a generic coil-spring independent front suspension.

Coil springs and adjustable shocks provide much more adjustability than torsion bars, and Mopar's front suspension geometry isn't exactly ideal for a Pro Touring build. That doesn't mean it's impossible to make a Mopar handle; it just means it costs a little more money and takes more time.

In most cases, the answer to these odd suspension configurations is to replace the entire setup with a more common design, such as a standard coil-spring front suspension. Detroit Speed's solution is called the X-Gen subframe, which can be adapted to

For the Mopar crowd, a true Pro Touring build is not easy. Many Mopar platforms featured torsion-bar front suspension and leaf-spring rear suspension, neither of which offer great handling in stock form. You can upgrade the torsion bars for an improved spring rate but at the end of the day, the poor suspension geometry is a big part of the handling problem.

Thinking outside the box certainly grabs more attention than a standard first-generation Camaro build. This Chevy Impala station wagon isn't the prime suspect for a Pro Touring build but there are plenty of performance parts available for this full-size platform. This car's crusty appearance adds to the cool factor!

Pickup trucks are also on the list of unconventional Pro Touring projects. Mark Turner didn't go all out on his green Chevy C-10 but the truck now handles much better than stock, and offers a comfortable ride. The same theories apply to the trucks: lower the center of gravity, reduce body roll, and increase traction.

many applications, from street rods to muscle cars. It's a generic 2 x 4–inch frame that ties into the existing front frame rails and features a race-proven front suspension geometry. It's available in 53.5- and 59.5-inch track widths to fit a wide range of vehicles, and provide big-time handling improvements.

End Results

Through the years, the Pro Touring movement has seen a number of wild combinations with one-off parts and head-turning looks. The Pro Touring bug has bitten a lot of gearheads around the world as evidenced by everything from pickup trucks with trick suspension to unassuming classic cars from the 1950s. Some folks are even taking traditional-style hot rods from the 1930s and making them into all-out handling machines with wide rubber, big brakes, and serious suspension setups. Thinking outside the box (or as *Hot Rod* magazine used to say "Dare to be Different") is a great option for folks who want to stand out from the crowd.

Regardless of the multitude of options for build platforms, most builds are centered on the muscle car era, and that is where Detroit Speed has focused its efforts. From the earliest beginnings, Detroit Speed built components for first-generation Camaros. Since then, Kyle and Stacy Tucker have turned their business into the most popular source for Pro

Hot Rod *magazine coined the phrase "Dare to be Different" a few decades ago and it has carried through to the modern era. In the Pro Touring world, this Studebaker is about as different as it gets but it shares many traits with mainstream Pro Touring cars, including a supercharged LS engine.*

Many enthusiasts are resorting to four-door and station wagon designs because the two-doors are harder to find, but the real advantage to these cars is space for all of your friends. This Chevy II wagon is a perfect Pro Touring example with its LS engine swap, big disc brakes, and aftermarket suspension.

Detroit Speed leads the way in the Pro Touring market, thanks to years of engineering experience and thousands of hours of research and development, as well as rigorous testing on and off the track. All components are manufactured in the United States, and each component serves a major purpose.

Touring components for many makes and models, including Camaro, Nova, Chevelle, Monte Carlo, Mustang, and Corvette.

Who Is Detroit Speed?

The evolution of a business is dependent on a number of factors, and it was Kyle and Stacy Tucker's passion to take a small backyard shop and turn it into a key player in the automotive aftermarket. The husband and wife team never imagined their efforts would catch on so quickly but the growth of their company speaks volumes for the quality and performance of each product. It certainly helps that Kyle and Stacy are hardcore enthusiasts, with the same desires that every gearhead possesses.

The early days of Detroit Speed remained in the two-car garage; Kyle and Stacy were the only employees. Starting small was the only option for this couple, but they eventually built a new shop and began hiring employees. Without question, the biggest shake-up in the company was the decision to move its operations from Michigan to Mooresville, North Carolina, in late 2004.

Although it was a risky decision for the Detroit Speed owners, the move offered more space, much cheaper operational costs, and access to one of the most racing-oriented towns in America, thanks to its deep roots in NASCAR racing.

Whether you buy a complete suspension kit or piece yours together with individual components from Detroit Speed, you'll reap the benefits of a race-proven design with the practicality of your everyday driver. Rear suspension kits are also available to bring the tired suspension into the modern era.

Many of the parts suppliers and manufacturers used for Detroit Speed products (JRi shocks, for instance) are based in Mooresville, so it offers a great convenience for the Detroit Speed crew. With many of the NASCAR race teams located in Mooresville, it also creates an abundance of talented car guys who provide outstanding skills in metalworking, welding, and machining.

Already established with valued employees, the move was no simple task, but it made the most sense on many levels. The employees of Detroit Speed were so passionate about their careers that they moved their families to North Carolina. That says a lot for the integrity of the company and the common desire among its employees to get bigger and better. Now the company operates in a 35,000-square-foot facility with 45 employees who handle sales, marketing, product manufacturing, car builds, and much more.

Kyle and Stacy Tucker are still heavily involved with the day-to-day operations at Detroit Speed, and you'll likely see them at many events every year, racing their "test cars," including the 1969 Camaro, 1970

The engineering process is extensive at Detroit Speed, and for good reason. Kyle and Stacy Tucker want their products to perform at the highest level possible. The parts have to be strong and 100 percent effective. Attention to detail put Detroit Speed's handcrafted products at the top of the food chain.

Just as they used The Twister *as a marketing tool, Kyle and Stacy Tucker continue to promote Detroit Speed by showing off their project vehicles. They call them "test cars," and use them at many autocross events across the country. These cars are always in the top of the running order!*

Camaro, 1963 Chevy II, 1965 Chevelle, and several others. They thrash on their cars, getting a true test of their components, and proving the performance potential to customers who might have thought the parts were just to make the car sit lower. At the end of the day, it is one of the best forms of marketing, but it's also enjoyable for Kyle and Stacy because driving these Pro Touring beasts is just as much fun as building them.

From day one, Detroit Speed has concentrated on functional products that provide real-world handling differences. It began with first-generation Camaros and later blossomed to many other platforms, most of which fall under the GM umbrella. However, Detroit Speed's recent efforts have been focused on Ford Mustang suspension, so they are certainly reaching out as the years roll on.

The goal with involving Detroit Speed in the making of this book is to give you the inside scoop on the components, while also coaching you through the installation and tuning process. Kyle Tucker is one of the best in the business, so when he agreed to share some of his chassis and suspension knowledge, it was a no-brainer, and *Detroit Speed's How to Build a Pro Touring Car* was born. If you're interested in building a Pro Touring car, keep reading for an in-depth view of the necessary steps to make it happen with your favorite muscle car.

Along with promoting the brand with high-tech Pro Touring cars, Detroit Speed has an awesome 18-wheeler setup that offers an up-close-and-personal look at its products. Detroit Speed travels to many Goodguys events, as well as many other events that cater to the Pro Touring crowd.

What started as a hobby for Kyle Tucker turned into a business venture, and the rest, as they say, is history. Detroit Speed is a leader in the automotive aftermarket industry, and this book is a guide to building your very own Pro Touring vehicle.

The Twister

Kyle and Stacy Tucker are fully immersed in the Pro Touring market but their initial efforts were prior to the market's rapid growth. The car was known as *The Twister* and it was based on a 1969 Camaro, one of the most popular Pro Touring platforms of all time.

The engineering that went into *The Twister* build was the result of minimal aftermarket product support. The Tuckers couldn't find any suspension components that met their needs so they decided to design their own and put them to use. It took two and a half years to build *The Twister* but when you consider that most of the suspension parts were built from scratch in Kyle's spare time, the overall build time frame was fairly quick. What Kyle didn't know was that his Camaro project would be the greatest marketing tool he could've created.

Making a first impression in the automotive aftermarket is a big step for building a business, and Detroit Speed's first build, *The Twister*, is a perfect example. The Tuckers set out to make it handle well, and as a result of their modifications, the car presented the textbook Pro Touring look. Large-diameter wheels with wide tires, a lowered stance, and trick suspension made it a standout at national events, and word quickly spread that it wasn't simply a show car; it was built to perform. This car had a fuel injected small-block, a manual transmission with overdrive, huge Baer disc brakes on all four corners, and even a roll cage. Most of these items were not standard street car equipment at the time, so the car had major wow factor. The bright yellow paint job was icing on the cake for this attention-getting machine.

Pro Touring had just started when Kyle and Stacy Tucker debuted The Twister, *a bright yellow 1969 Camaro that turned the hot rodding world on its ear. Kyle and Stacy built it from the ground up, and used the car as the ultimate marketing tool for their up-and-coming business.*

The Twister Camaro debuted on the Hot Rod Power Tour in the summer of 2000. Everyone loved the car, and the fact that it functioned well and looked great garnered lots of attention from magazines including *Car Craft, Chevy High Performance, Hot Rod,* and *Super Rod.* A few short months after *The Twister* made its way to several events, the phone was ringing off the hook with folks who were interested in everything from complete builds to individual components.

With the amount of magazine exposure created by the first build, the Tuckers saw a great demand in the market and took it to the next level. Kyle was so driven by the success of his Camaro build that he took a leave of absence at General Motors in December 2000, starting Detroit Speed, Inc. out of

Under the hood of The Twister *is a 406-ci small-block Chevy engine, outfitted with aluminum heads and a tuned-port fuel injection system. Also notable is the Vintage Air A/C system, which made the car's debut at the Hot Rod Power Tour a comfortable weeklong journey.*

Inside, black and white hound's-tooth covers modified Recaro bucket seats; a custom dash and gauge panel provide a fresh take on a classic 1969 Camaro interior. One of the biggest wow factors of this Pro Touring machine was its full roll cage and safety harnesses, something rarely seen in a street-driven car at the time.

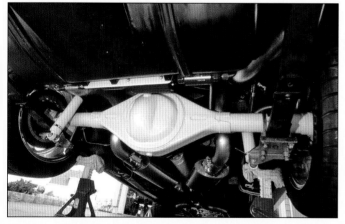

Out back, The Twister *featured a Ford 9-inch-style rear end, similar to the ones used in NASCAR racing, suspended by leaf springs. Although most high-end Pro Touring cars currently use a four-link suspension with coil-overs, Kyle's original leaf-spring setup was hot at the time. He moved the springs inboard and widened the original wheel tubs to fit the larger tires.*

Another feature that rocked the automotive aftermarket involved the massive rear tires that rolled beneath The Twister *Camaro. Although small compared to some of the Pro Touring builds you see today, these tires kicked off a trend of mini-tubbed muscle cars with super-wide low-profile rubber.*

his two-car garage. Kyle's boss offered to restore his position if things didn't work out with the new business idea, while Stacy kept her engineering job at General Motors during this time. It was only a couple years before business picked up to the point of Stacy saying good-bye to General Motors and taking on full-time duties at Detroit Speed. ■

You may notice several differences in this front suspension compared to what is currently offered by Detroit Speed. Kyle's original front suspension setup consisted of custom tubular upper control arms, modified original stamped-steel lower control arms, a custom spindle, and a custom spring and shock configuration. Also note the large sway bar and disc brakes.

As if the bright yellow paint job weren't enough, The Twister *featured a lowered stance and wide tires and wheels on all four corners. When Kyle and Stacy Tucker drove this car all over the country in 2000, it put Detroit Speed on the map, and the couple never looked back.*

SKILLS, TECHNIQUES AND TOOLS

So you've made the decision to go the Pro Touring route with your vehicle. Let's get down to business regarding the necessary tools and skills to get the job done. Tackling a restoration or custom build is an in-depth process that shouldn't be taken lightly. Some special tools are necessary, and if you've never torn into a muscle car, you'll learn a lot during the build. This book, with its great collection of photos, tips, and

special tricks, should help you build an awesome Pro Touring vehicle.

First of all, a good mechanical mind-set is necessary to perform many of these installations. Even if you've never restored or modified a car, the process is fairly straightforward if you use some common sense and a basic set of tools. The techniques are sometimes tricky but tips are provided that allow you to complete a Pro Touring build in your

garage. You may not be interested in taking on such a daunting task but even if you send your car to a professional shop, it's a good idea to know the ins and outs of your build before you hand it over.

Who Can Build a Pro Touring Car?

The ability to build a Pro Touring car depends on the extent of the build and your experience level. If your only automotive experience is

If you're a car guy, an empty engine bay isn't all that scary. But if you're new to the hobby, this could offer enough intimidation to turn you away. Luckily, the right tools make a huge difference and make big projects easy to tackle.

A full assortment of regular hand tools is a must for any car build, including a Pro Touring project. Don't overlook the obvious stuff, such as wrenches, sockets, and hammers. This stuff gets used a lot during the build process.

Specialized tools, such as this bushing remover/installer (used for GM A-Body upper rear axle bushings), really come in handy when you're in the heat of the battle. When a hammer and chisel don't get the job done, a specialized tool will help.

changing the oil in your daily driver, you may not want to start from scratch with a complete build. Don't be afraid to take on a challenging task but know your limitations, especially if welding or other modifications are involved in your plan.

Luckily, the key components in a Pro Touring build consist of suspension parts, and most of them are bolt-on pieces. An average car guy with a full set of hand tools can easily rebuild the suspension and add a few aftermarket parts along the way.

If you're going all out with items such as a mini-tub kit or a Detroit Speed QUADRALink rear suspension, you'll do a fair amount of cutting, welding, and grinding to install the components.

If this is your first build, there will certainly be moments that make you think, "Can I really do this?" and that's perfectly fine. If this stuff were easy, you wouldn't need to read a book about it. The main thing to remember is the wealth of information in this book, as well as the helpful

nature of most car guys. If you have a couple of gearhead buddies, don't be afraid to ask for help. You'd be surprised how much more quickly and easily things may fall together with another pair of hands and eyeballs. Missed steps are often avoided when a helping hand is involved, and to be perfectly honest, it's much more fun to hang out in the shop with a couple of friends than to handle the build alone. Go ahead and plan on ordering a few pizzas and stocking up on cold beverages. Your friends will likely accept this as an even trade for their time and experience. If not, you need to find some new friends or take on an easier project!

All joking aside, you will most definitely need help from time to time. Some of the suspension pieces are a handful, and you always want an extra pair of hands when it's time to lift heavy stuff, such as the rear end or subframe, or attempt to install an engine and transmission. Just as there are times you need a helping hand, you may also need to have

Rotisseries are an excellent way to reach every square inch of your project car but please note that they are not completely necessary. If you have a vehicle torn down far enough to put on a rotisserie, you're already pretty deep into the project.

Simple things can sometimes bog you down, but remember that a floor jack and hand tools can accomplish a lot of tasks in the garage. Jack stands are an absolute must, and an extra floor jack may provide assistance in some situations.

Do-it-yourselfers go to great lengths to build cars that are out of the ordinary and they're also a staple of the Pro Touring industry. If you're willing to cut, weld, grind, and hammer on a car to make it all come together, you're ready to dive headfirst into a Pro Touring build.

If you've ever built your own engine, you certainly qualify to build a Pro Touring car. Even if it was a lawn mower engine, you've exhibited the necessary mechanical common sense. Some aspects are simply bolting parts together, though others require additional skills.

certain items pressed into place, which may require some running around town to find a shop that can help. Control-arm bushings, some types of ball joints, and most leaf-spring bushings are usually the only items that require a press to disassemble and install the new parts, so it usually isn't a big expense or time consumer. With this in mind, the extent of your build determines how much time you spend at the local fab shop or machine shop. Engine builds

can be costly and sometimes risky for a novice but it's part of the process, unless you have the available cash for a ready-to-run crate engine.

Cash is another subject that should be covered because not everyone is ready to spend thousands of dollars on an old car. The beauty of building a Pro Touring car is that you can get the right look without spending an inordinate amount of money right off the bat. A lowered stance, large-diameter wheels, performance

tires, and a couple of engine modifications would provide a great start. Then you can upgrade items one at a time, as funds become available. In the meantime, you can still enjoy your car and keep it on the road.

This approach is okay for a budget builder, as long as the necessary steps are taken to make sure the car is safe to drive during the upgrading process. You wouldn't want to take off down the road in a Camaro that hasn't received any suspension or brake work in 20 years, so be cautious, and spend your money wisely. In other words, make sure the car is safe before you start spending money on modifications.

Many car guys would rather take on the entire project at once, instead of the piecemeal approach. Full-on gearheads take a car completely down to the bare bones and bring it back up from scratch. Be prepared for lots of down time if you take this approach. Jobs, family, and regular everyday life certainly get in the way of progress, so

Not everyone can afford to install a lift in his or her garage (sometimes space is the real issue) and it's not a mandatory piece of equipment for the average car guy. It definitely makes suspension work a lot easier to handle but it's a matter of convenience, not necessity.

Regardless of your budget or skill level, sparks are going to fly if you take on a Pro Touring build, so safety is a top priority to protect your eyes, skin, and hearing. Unless you buy a completed car and bolt on some mild components, you need to brush up on your welding, cutting, and grinding skills. In most cases, a MIG welder is sufficient for the average build.

TIG welding is highly preferred in many aspects but it's not the only form of welding that gets the job done. TIG welding is a little trickier than MIG, but as long as you know what you're doing, it's super strong and it lays down nice and flat.

don't expect to completely rebuild a classic muscle car in a few months. Sometimes it takes years to accomplish the goal but it's worth every penny and every hour spent when you slide behind the wheel with confidence that your car will handle whatever you throw at it.

Where Can a Pro Touring Car Be Built?

A Pro Touring car can be built in your driveway but it's easier if you have a well-equipped shop, where the car can sit in the dry and remain disassembled for a while. Although

Kyle and Stacy Tucker built their first Camaro in a small two-car home garage, you'd be better off in a larger setting because a car takes up much more room when it's scattered into a thousand pieces. The last thing you want to do is move your wife's car and your lawn mower outdoors

Some of the most awesome Pro Touring machines have been built in the attached garage of someone's house. Although it isn't the ideal location for a full-on build, it's how Kyle and Stacy Tucker started. Full builds are tough in the tight confines of a home garage but minor repairs and modifications are easily achieved.

A chassis table is something most car guys never use, unless they work in a professional chassis or fab shop. These tables are very useful for squaring up a chassis but it's rare that the average shop has enough room for a bulky rig that takes up as much space as the entire car.

It's amazing how much space is needed when you tear a car completely down to the bare body and frame. Even a moderately sized garage (this is a 30 x 50–foot example) quickly fills to capacity when a car is scattered into a million pieces.

Suspension upgrades can sometimes be as simple as unbolting the original component and bolting the new one into place. Regardless of the severity of the build, you need plenty of room to get around and underneath the car.

while your project car is temporarily disabled, but that's not to say it hasn't been done against the will of wives around the world.

Some folks say that an automotive lift, such as a two- or four-post unit, is necessary for a complete build. Although a lift certainly makes it easy to get beneath your car, it's not a deal breaker if your shop isn't large enough for it. Lots of incredible Pro Touring cars have been built in small garages with nothing more than a floor jack and an assortment of jack stands. In fact, Detroit Speed often uses wooden lift blocks and jack stands under their builds, as this brings the car off the ground while also allowing plenty of room to get in it, under it, and around it.

Regardless of the size of your shop, be prepared for an influx of junk filling every corner. Disassembling a car, especially when you have plans to replace many of the parts, creates quite a swap-meet pile. Some guys like to keep the original parts, in the event they decide to go back to stock, but here is a little secret: When

you realize how well your muscle car handles with the Pro Touring treatment, you'll never want to go back!

Swap meets are a great way to recoup some of your spending, and it clears out space in the shop, so maybe then you can get your lawn mower out of the rain. Swap meets are also a great place to find parts on the cheap. Here's a thought: Just buy

A must-have in the shop is a level. It doesn't have to be fancy or high-dollar; just a basic level from the hardware store. A level and a tape measure have been instrumental tools in the automotive world. If you have a smart phone, you can get an application that offers a level, which really comes in handy!

a cover for the mower and reserve the room in the shop for more car parts.

What Tools Are Needed?

It's always important to remember safety when working beneath a car, so if you plan to do the suspension and undercarriage work without a lift, be sure to use a high-quality

Hammers, dollies, chisels, and punches rank highly on the list of must-have tools. Any tool that is used for hammering or driving something into place needs to be a high-quality piece. Don't get caught up in the luster of cheap tools; get the good stuff, and it'll last forever.

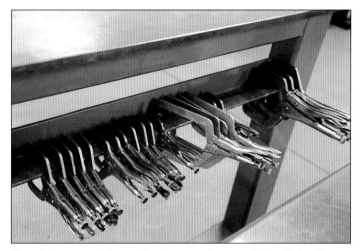

You'll always wish you had a couple more Vise-Grips in your toolbox. Regular Vise-Grip pliers come in handy for just about anything, but special ones, such as these C-clamp pliers, can do the work of three of your friends trying to hold that panel in place.

If you're going to do anything more than simply bolting on aftermarket components, you need to invest in a good welder. MIG welders are affordable and easy to use, whereas TIG machines require a little more expertise and a bit more money.

A good collection of hammers is necessary for any car build. Dead-blow hammers are great for whacking on parts that need a delicate touch, but you should have a mini-sledge at your disposal for when things get serious.

Shown here are two great tools for anyone who plans to work with metal. A bench grinder is one of the cheapest and handiest tools ever, although the drill press saves lots of time and effort, compared to using a hand drill.

Sometimes a hand drill is the only option, so put a cordless drill on your wish list. Another tool that is super convenient is a cordless impact wrench. The battery life is great in most cases, and it takes a lot of the effort out of loosening and tightening bolts.

floor jack and jack stands. Never slide under a car without giving it a good nudge on the jack stands to make sure it's steady. You can never be too safe in this situation. Never use concrete cinder blocks as jack stands. They work great for the foundation of your house but they are not meant to hold the weight of a car.

There isn't a designated list of necessary tools to perform a Pro Touring build because each build requires a different approach. Some

builds are quite simple, with only bolt-on additions, whereas others are very extensive with lots of cutting, welding, and custom fabrication. Both ends of the spectrum are covered, with the build-up featured in this book; it includes a great mix of bolt-on components and hand-fabbed goodies. Obviously, the fabrication aspect of a custom build requires a number of specialty tools, but it's a simple matter of how far you want to take it.

Air tools are a must for any complete build but you can get by with a good assortment of regular hand tools if you're making simple upgrades to the suspension, brakes, or steering system. If you're digging into the engine and drivetrain, specialty tools are must-have items. Some of the most-used tools in the shop are clamping pliers of all shapes and sizes, a big hammer, and a few cordless power tools, such as an impact drill and reciprocating saw.

If you're planning to plumb the braking system or fuel system using hard line, you need a good hand bender. Bending lines over your knee sometimes works but hand benders are cheap and a little more precise than just eyeballing it and hoping for the best.

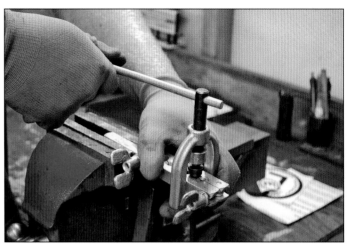

A tubing flare tool is also a must-have for fabricating hard lines for the braking or fuel system. You may not use this tool every day but it will prove its worth many times over. Flaring tools are generally cheap enough to add to your tool collection even if you plan to use them only once.

Electric tools, such as grinders, drills, and saws, are also important items to have; many of them can take the place of air tools if you do not have an adequate air compressor. In many instances, one of these tools will get you out of a bind that a regular hand tool just can't handle. Be sure to have plenty of drop cord with the correct gauge of wire (12-gauge is suggested for all power tools) for this sort of project, and always keep a shop light handy. If you're willing to throw in some extra cash, you could always opt for cordless tools. Even if you have air tools and an assortment of electric tools, a cordless impact belongs on the must-have list.

A good welder should be on every wish list; a MIG welder is sufficient for almost any project. Although most professional shops use a TIG welder for items such as roll-cage tubing, it isn't the most practical machine for the novice welder. You can pick up a MIG welder without breaking the bank, and it really comes in handy if you like the idea of making your own brackets or repairing sheet metal. Most cheap MIG welders are

One of the most versatile and simplistic tools is a vise. You'll use it every day, whether it's clamping something in place to make a cut, tighten a bolt, or weld two pieces together. It also serves as a great anvil.

You may not see the need to invest in a hydraulic press if you plan to build only one car every five years but it sure saves a lot of time when it comes to suspension components. Ball joints and control-arm bushings are generally pressed-in items, so having a press in the shop saves time.

Mild or Wild?

A mild build may consist of minor upgrades to the suspension and drivetrain but no big tasks that require fabrication or major welding. These types of builds are generally short-term projects that keep your vehicle up and rolling, instead of torn apart in the corner of your garage.

Even though this Camaro's subframe is nicely detailed, it isn't overly complicated, and it gives the car a great stance. The owner is leaving a lot of handling performance on the table by retaining the stock control arms (because of the unwanted flex from the stamped-steel arms and the poor geometry) but the aftermarket coil springs, larger sway bar, and new bushings help tremendously.

You probably have tons of ideas floating around in your head regarding your dream Pro Touring build. Regardless of whether the dream build is realistic, you should determine the extent of your build before you jump in. It's important to know your limits; choosing between mild and wild can sometimes be a tough decision, especially if you are confident of your abilities. Sometimes it's a matter of budget and sometimes it's a matter of practicality when the car is completed. The choice is yours and the door is wide open for all sorts of great combinations of aftermarket components.

New springs, shocks, sway bars, and maybe an upgraded set of brakes can totally change the way a muscle car handles, so that may be the extent of your build. If so, you'll likely enjoy the difference in performance, but hard-core guys want to continually get faster, and that's when wild combinations are created. A truly wild build will likely have a big price tag because of the high-end parts as well as the labor costs involved in a professional build. But that's not to say that a high-end car can't be built in a home garage without the use of high-tech equipment.

The following is a comparison between a mild build and a wild build.

Anytime a car is stripped to the bare metal, and multiple panels are replaced, you're looking at a long-term project. Custom fabrication takes time if you're doing it yourself, and money if you're hiring it out, so high-end builds add up quickly.

A full roll cage with racing seats is a good sign of an all-out Pro Touring build. Roll cages offer great rigidity to the chassis, but actually create a hazard if you plan to drive on the street. Even a tiny fender bender could slam your unprotected noggin against the tubing.

Mild or Wild? *CONTINUED*

Mild

Chassis and Suspension

Subframe connectors
Front suspension rebuild
  (new ball joints, tie-rods, control-arm bushings)
New coil springs with appropriate spring rate and ride height
High-quality shock absorbers (front and rear)
Larger anti-roll bar
New Pitman arm and idler arm
Disc brake upgrade
New leaf springs with appropriate ride height
17 x 8–inch wheels with generic street tires

Engine and Drivetrain

Aluminum intake manifold
Performance carburetor
Mild camshaft and lifter upgrade
Headers and exhaust
Aluminum radiator and electric fan(s)
Overdrive transmission

Wild

Chassis and Suspension

Subframe connectors
Detroit Speed hydroformed subframe assembly
Tubular control arms
Adjustable coil-over conversion (front and rear)
Splined anti-roll bar
Rack-and-pinion steering
Large-diameter brakes with six-piston calipers
Four-link rear suspension
Roll cage
18 x 10 and 18 x 12 wheels and high-performance tires

Engine and Drivetrain

LS engine swap
High-performance oiling system
Aftermarket cylinder heads and valvetrain
High-performance camshaft and lifters
Custom engine control module (ECM) and wiring harness
Complete fuel system
LS swap headers and custom exhaust
Aluminum radiator and electric fan(s)
Overdrive transmission (with high-performance clutch set)
Rear-end gears with appropriate ratio ■

not suitable for welding thick steel, such as the material used on chassis and suspension components, but it's certainly a must-have tool if you're planning to rebuild a car.

For some of the detail-oriented portions of a Pro Touring build, such as wiring, plumbing, and the like, you need a few specialty tools. For brake lines and fuel lines you need a small tubing bender and a flare tool. You can always buy a brake line or fuel line kit but it's much cleaner if you bend the lines and route them to your liking. As for wiring, you need cutters, strippers, and crimping tools, along with a soldering iron, a good continuity tester, and a lot of patience.

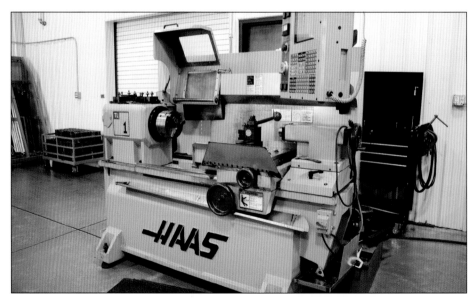

If money and space aren't an issue, a big lathe can be a lot of fun. Obviously, this isn't the average tool for a Pro Touring build, but if you have machining experience you can certainly crank out some cool stuff.

CHASSIS

As mentioned in earlier chapters, the stiffness and strength of the components play a large role in making a car handle and perform well. The same can be said for the vehicle's chassis and body structure, which is the backbone of the entire system. If the chassis isn't strong enough to support the abuse, you may be leaving a lot of performance on the table, even with high-dollar suspension components. That's why it's important to prepare your car's frame or unibody structure for hard cornering, hard braking, and hard acceleration.

First things first: You must always start with a rust-free car. A little rust in the front fenders or, maybe, in the quarter panels isn't an area of concern, but any time you see a vehicle with rusted floorpans, trunkpan, or rocker panels it's best to stay away. If there is significant rust in these areas, it likely means that the chassis structure has been affected by rust also. Regardless of the chassis configuration (full frame or unibody), rust weakens the metal significantly and creates all sorts of problems down the road. For West Coast guys this isn't usually an issue but any car guy east of the Mississippi River has dealt with rust at some point in his life.

It's never a good idea to start with a total rust bucket, unless you plan on gutting the body and sitting it over a custom tube chassis. At that point, the body is just a shell and the chassis is brand-new so rust is no longer a concern. Obviously, it takes a special breed of car guy to go all out on a tube chassis Pro Touring build. But trust me it's been done.

Body-On-Frame

If you're building a truck, a Corvette, or a GM A-, B-, or G-Body, you're dealing with a vehicle with a body-on-frame configuration. That means the chassis is a separate structure from the body, which is an ideal setup in terms of strength. This full frame can also be affected by rust but it isn't nearly as fragile as the chassis structure of a unibody design. Full-frame cars are generally heavier than unibody cars but provide a great platform to build upon.

The automobile was originally designed with a body-on-frame configuration. By the 1960s, many manufacturers were making the switch to unibody designs, maintaining the body-on-frame design only with larger cars. For General Motors, the B-Body (Impala and other similar models), A-Body (Chevelle), and G-Body (Monte Carlo) featured a full frame.

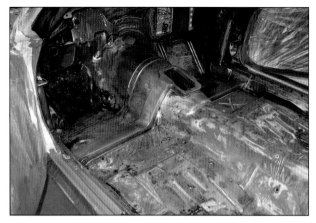

This is an example of a very clean, rust-free, second-generation Camaro. The floorpans, trunk pans, and quarter panels are common rust-prone areas, and they are important parts of the car's structure because the Camaro features a unibody construction.

It's always important to do a "cross out" measurement to make sure the unibody is square. This involves choosing four equal reference points (body mount bolts suffice if you cannot locate the original "gauge holes"). Using a tram gauge or plumb bobs, measure diagonally, and compare the two measurements. As long as the reference points are equal, the measurements should be very close. Factory tolerance is 1/8 inch, so if the numbers are within 1/4 inch, consider yourself lucky!

The strength of the body-on-frame design is undoubtedly the highlight of this design but many applications still require additional bracing to keep the structure solid and stiff. Early Chevy Impalas (1958–1964), for instance, feature an X-frame design, as opposed to the more generic perimeter design of many other makes and models. Don't ask why General Motors thought this was a good idea but the X-frame certainly doesn't lend itself well to high-performance driving.

Moving on through the years, General Motors stepped up its game with the A-Body platform but it took the perimeter design a bit too far by building a strong structure around the perimeter of the car. This leaves a lot to be desired in the crossmember and bracing department, making for a frame that flexes during harsh driving conditions. For most full-frame cars (especially the GM A-Bodies) additional chassis braces are necessary. Luckily, they are widely available to fit the popular 1964–1972 GM midsize models.

In most cases you can spot a full-frame car just by the size of it. Ford and General Motors placed full-size models (Impala, Bonneville, Galaxie, and Monterey, among others) on a full frame, based on the weight of the vehicle. They felt the

If rust or chassis damage is an issue for your project, you can always opt for aftermarket components to repair the damaged metal. Of course, this requires some intense fabrication and welding skills, depending on the severity of the damage. For chassis and floor repairs, a MIG welder is preferred for its ease of use. Starting with a rust-free car is ideal.

When General Motors introduced the A-Body platform in 1964, it was the backbone of the first string of muscle cars. The Chevelle, GTO, 442, and GS shared the same chassis, which featured a multi-link rear suspension and a perimeter-style frame. This design leaves a lot to be desired because of a lack of bracing around the suspension mounting points but it's a strong platform to build upon.

Corvettes can sometimes be confusing to the novice because they were not technically a muscle car or a pony car. They were considered a sports car, and they featured a body-on-frame design from day one. Corvettes also featured a fiberglass body from day one, and an independent rear suspension starting in 1963.

heavier car needed a full frame to support it, and they were right.

Chrysler Corporation didn't play into this mindset, choosing unibody construction for most of its models, starting in 1960. The heavy weight, along with metal deterioration caused by rust, spelled disaster for many Mopars from the 1960s and 1970s, which is part of the reason they're worth so much money. There aren't many of them left!

Despite the original flaws and deterioration after years of use, full-frame vehicles provide the necessary strength for a bulletproof Pro Touring build. You may need to strengthen a few points on the frame, especially the areas around the suspension mounting points, but you'll save quite a bit of time and money

on things such as subframe connectors, shock tower braces, etc., on a full-frame design.

The weakest points in a full frame are usually located around the "kick up" where the frame rails go over the rear-end housing. These joints can sometimes flex, and they are susceptible to rust, which causes the joints to weaken even further. For the suspension to do its job, the mounting points must be capable of taking the stress of harsh driving without flexing, as even 1/16 inch of flex can cause changes in the geometry. Unfortunately, full-frame cars are not the norm in the Pro Touring world, so most folks have to spend a lot of time and money to make their unibody vehicle as sturdy as a body-on-frame vehicle.

With this in mind, a number of enthusiasts have built custom frames for cars that originally used unibody construction. This is a major task, as it usually requires the removal of all floorpans and trunk pans to even get started on a custom chassis. Then new pans must be fabricated to work with the chassis, and this usually leads to the original result of full-frame cars: extra weight. It certainly isn't a beginner's project. The end result is usually a full-on race car, instead of a practical Pro Touring vehicle that you can legitimately drive on the street.

Unibody

Until the 1960s almost all American auto manufacturers used the body-on-frame configuration, even though Nash introduced the first successful unibody car in 1941 after a somewhat flawed attempt by Chrysler almost a decade earlier. The term "unibody" is actually short for unit body, which actually means unitary construction. This type of construction means that the body and chassis are essentially the same unit.

With a unibody design, the floorpans, rocker panels, and inner fenders are part of the vehicle's chassis structure. With most muscle car and pony car applications tipping the scales at

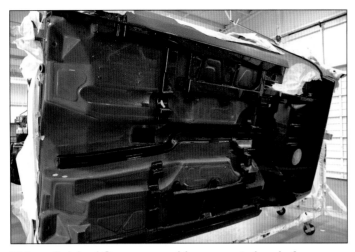

This unfinished Camaro provides a great visual of a unibody chassis construction. The satin parts are essentially just sheet metal, used for the floorpans, trunk pans, etc.; the glossy portions are structural components. This example has been modified with subframe connectors and other structural bracing.

General Motors is the only manufacturer that used a bolt-in front subframe. The frame unbolts from the chassis, unlike the Ford and Chrysler unibodies that feature a welded front frame section. This removable subframe makes for easy assembly but suffers from a bit more flex due to the movement of the bolts and bushings.

3,000 pounds or more, that is a lot of weight to be supported by sheet metal. The advantage of unibody construction for auto manufacturers was weight savings and ease of construction at the assembly plant. Generally, the car would technically have frame rails on the front and rear of the vehicle but these rails would be welded directly to the floorpan and cowl area. General Motors was the exception with its bolt-on front subframes.

It wasn't until the late 1950s that Ford adopted this chassis design for its larger cars, such as the Lincoln and Ford Thunderbird. From there the trend grew, and Ford used a unibody construction on other models, including the Falcon, Mustang, and Torino (which was changed to body-on-frame in 1972). Ford passenger cars have always been plagued with minimal engine bay real estate, thanks to huge shock towers. It is a major chore to stuff a large engine into any early Mustang, Falcon, or Fairlane without doing major work to the front suspension.

Detroit Speed's new Aluma-Frame for 1964–1970 Mustangs is a bolt-in front suspension module that replaces the original front suspension and removes the shock towers altogether. The Aluma-Frame retains the original front subframe rails and provides lots of great advantages, including improved suspension geometry, rack-and-pinion steering, and adequate engine bay clearance for many modern power plants. (Read more about this front suspension system and how it helps Mustang guys enter the Pro Touring world in Chapter 4.)

General Motors jumped onto the unibody bandwagon when it introduced the Chevrolet Corvair in 1960. Although the Corvair was a totally different animal with its four-wheel independent suspension and rear-mounted engine, it served as the first of many unibody vehicles built by the General.

Two years later, the Chevy II was introduced; it was a much more conventional compact car for the time. It, unlike any other vehicles at the time, had a bolt-on front subframe that was obviously a manufacturing decision designed to save the company time and money. But, hey, it turned out to be a great move for Pro Touring guys because it allows easy subframe removal and installation. A few bolts here and there, and the entire front end of the car can be removed. Brilliant.

When General Motors joined the "pony car" market in 1967 with the Camaro and Firebird, it introduced its F-Body chassis design, which has turned into the most popular Pro Touring platform in the industry. The F-Body continued the bolt-on front subframe approach, and later passed it on to the 1968–1974 Chevy Nova, and BOP (Buick, Oldsmobile, Pontiac) equivalents.

As mentioned earlier, Mopar used unibody chassis construction for many years, even on its full-size cars. When the muscle car and pony car craze hit in the mid-to-late 1960s, Mopar had a number of high-performance models, all of which

Chrysler Corporation relied heavily on the unibody platform, but its chassis designs featured an integrated front and rear frame section. Large cars, such as this Dodge Charger, are a little too heavy for high-performance handling without first installing additional bracing and subframe connectors.

Ford also used an integrated front and rear subframe. This Ford Mustang has the floorpan removed for rust repair, which shows exactly how much this chassis relies on the structure of the sheet-metal floorpan. This chassis is greatly strengthened by extending these front subframe rails to meet the rear rails.

Subframe connectors are pretty simple pieces of metal but they're very important chassis components. If you're serious about building a Pro Touring car with a unibody chassis, a pair of weld-in subframe connectors is a must-do modification to take advantage of the new suspension.

featured a unibody construction with torsion-bar front suspension and leaf-spring rear suspension, a common design element in most of its models in the Chrysler, Dodge, and Plymouth lines.

The Mopar crowd doesn't get much love in the Pro Touring world but many of the Mopars from the 1960s and early 1970s are very capable performers. It's just a matter of strengthening the unibody structure with subframe connectors and adding a mild roll cage to have a great platform to build upon. Aftermarket support for Mopars isn't quite up to par with the GM brands but if you're willing to shell out some dough for custom components, you can make a Mopar handle with the best of them.

Subframe Connectors

Despite the difference between the Big Three's attempts at unibody construction, they all share the same problem: strength and rigidity in harsh driving conditions. Drag racers and road racers deal with the same struggles when dealing with unibody cars, so the idea is to remove the tendency for the chassis to flex under hard loads. The answer, in most cases, involves fabricating or installing a set of subframe connectors. The connectors are self-explanatory, connecting the front portion of the frame rails to the rear portion of the frame rails. In other words, they provide support in the middle floorpan area, where manufacturers relied solely on the floorpan and rocker panel structure to take the abuse.

Luckily, subframe connectors are usually an easy install. Some are bolt-in style, suitable for a guy building a car in his driveway, but they tend to hang below the rocker panel

---

You hardly notice the subframe connectors when they are installed but they offer a great advantage over the stock unibody layout. Bolt-in connectors are available but they generally hang below the floor, which looks a bit tacky, and lack the strength of weld-in connectors. These through-floor subframe connectors require a bit more work but they work nicely and look great.

A full roll cage may not be necessary in your Pro Touring machine but a simple four-point roll bar can offer many advantages. It provides additional chassis stiffening, and it provides a safe mounting location for the five-point safety harnesses.

pinch weld to avoid the dips and pockets in the stock floorpan. This obviously isn't the most attractive look, so most hardcore Pro Touring enthusiasts go with a weld-in design that is recessed into the floorpan.

Weld-in connectors are a bit more work but it's totally worth the effort because they look a lot better and they provide much more strength. Weld-in subframe connectors essentially make the unibody as strong as a full-frame car, as long as all of the suspension mounting-points are rust-free. Weld-in subframe connectors provide definite advantages but also make GM's bolt-on front subframe a bit more permanent.

Subframe connectors are very important although they will add a few pounds to your car. With heavy-duty components comes extra weight. The additional pounds are offset by the strength of the unibody structure, and you'll still come in lighter than a full-frame car from the same era.

Roll Cage

There was a time when a roll bar or roll cage was used only in a serious race car. Times have certainly changed; many Pro Touring builds feature a mild roll bar, which provides safety, as well as additional strength for the unibody structure. Roll bars also offer a great mounting point for five-point safety harnesses. They have therefore become commonplace on Pro Touring cars and trucks.

If you've seen the interior of an all-out race car, you've seen the maze of round tubing that makes the roll cage. This jungle gym isn't practical, even for occasional street driving, because it's a hassle to get in and out of the car, and it also creates a serious hazard. (A roll cage creates a hazard; that's sort of ironic, right?) When you consider the extensive tubing, and the fact that it is designed to protect a driver who is wearing a helmet, the danger might become a little clearer.

Even a small collision in the parking lot could slam your head against one of the bars, which is never a good situation. Always take great precautions when driving a caged vehicle on the street. Even though it's ugly, roll-bar padding may be your best bet to protect your noggin.

The simpler four-point roll bars that are generally used in mild Pro Touring cars are less dangerous on the street. They're also fairly easy to install because they don't require nearly as much fabrication and installation time. Prefab kits are pretty common and easy to install, thanks to the bends, notches, and cuts being in all the right places from the get-go.

Most prefab four-point roll bars do not pass tech at NHRA- or IHRA-sanctioned drag strips. These drag racing organizations require a minimum of five roll-bar mounting points for cars that run quicker than 11.50 seconds in the quarter-mile. If you're building a multipurpose

As with any aspect of a Pro Touring build, it's easy to get carried away with the roll cage, such as on this Chevy II. Door bars are necessary in some racing organizations but they are overkill on a standard Pro Touring machine. Unless you're a serious racer, you'll hate climbing in and out of a jungle gym.

On a body-on-frame platform, the roll cage must go through the floorpans and weld directly to the frame rails. For unibody designs, the roll cage tubing must be attached to a 6 x 6–inch steel plate, which is first welded to the floorpan.

car, this is a very important detail to consider.

The NHRA rulebook also provides some great guidelines that translate to Pro Touring cars, while relating to the average car guy. It designates that roll bars on all body-on-frame cars must be connected to the frame (not to the floorpan). It also states that all roll bars in unibody cars must be attached to the car using 6 x 6–inch steel plates welded to the floorpan. These plates strengthen the mounting point for the roll bar and provide additional rigidity, allowing you to get the most out of the aftermarket suspension components.

If you're serious about road racing, refer to the Sports Car Club of America (SCCA) rulebook for exact rules on tubing sizes, appropriate mounting configurations, and other regulations. The SCCA is very strict on all of its rules but if you can pass SCCA tech, you're good to go with pretty much any racetrack or racing organization.

Mini-Tubs

Chassis modifications are plentiful in a typical Pro Touring build, and one of the most popular is to widen the original rear wheel tubs or install new tubs. The wheel tub (also known as the wheelhouse or wheelwell) is usually the limiting factor of tire and

wheel fitment on muscle cars and pony cars from the 1960s and 1970s.

The largest tire you can fit on a stock first-generation GM F-Body (Camaro or Firebird), for instance, is a 275/40R17 on a 17 x 9.5–inch wheel with 5.0- to 5.5-inch backspacing. Although this is a much larger tire and wheel than the original setup, the desire for larger rear tires is a common thread in the Pro Touring scene. By widening the tubs or installing a prefab mini-tub kit, you gain lots of real estate, allowing you to install larger rear tires for increased traction.

Detroit Speed offers wide tubs for most common GM applications, as well as complete mini-tub kits for leaf-spring cars. The installation process for wheel tubs requires a great deal of work, as the original tubs must be removed by drilling out the spot-welds. Next, the necessary cuts must be made to fit the new tubs into place, and then they can be plug-welded to the car.

Although a pair of widened tubs gains you some necessary room, you also have to consider the location of the original leaf springs if you're planning to utilize them on your car. If you're swapping to a custom rear suspension system, such as Detroit

Although Chevrolet continues to be the make of choice for Pro Touring builders, they are cursed with small wheel tubs. An F-Body (Camaro or Firebird) only holds a 275/40R17, and early Chevy II/Nova platforms are even more limited. Mini-tubs are a must if you want wide tires!

Speed's QUADRALink, leaf springs are the least of your worries.

If you're keeping the springs, you need offset shackles to move the springs inboard and free up the valuable space for rear tires and wheels. Moving the leaf springs inboard interferes with the original fuel tank location on a GM F-Body, but Detroit Speed offers narrowed fuel tanks for this purpose.

According to Detroit Speed, its mini-tubs and mini-tub kits provide enough room for a 335/30R18 tire, mounted to an 18 x 12–inch wheel on a 1969 F-Body. For the Chevy II crowd, Detroit Speed's mini-tubs allow for 10-inch-wide wheels and 295 tires on 1962–1965 models and an 11-inch wheel and 315 tire on the 1966–1967 models. If you have dealt with tire and wheel fitment on a Chevy II, this is a major improvement! Ford guys can also rejoice because mini-tubs for a Mustang can give it enough room for 10.5- to 12-inch wheels and 295 to 335 tires, depending on the year of the car.

This increased footprint certainly helps in the traction department, and it's just plain cool looking, regardless of the application.

This is a 1968 Camaro with stock tubs. The rear tires are 235/45R17s, mounted to 17 x 8–inch wheels. It offers a great look for a mild-mannered Pro Touring build but most folks want a much wider tire and wheel combination out back.

On the other side of the coin, this 1969 Camaro features a Detroit Speed mini-tub kit to squeeze a set of 335/30R20 tires into the rear tubs. A massive combination like this also requires a narrowed rear end to achieve the "deep dish" wheel look.

Project: Deep Tubs Installation

Detroit Speed forms its mini-tubs in-house for all popular applications. Installing them is a pretty involved process that includes a substantial amount of cutting, grinding, and welding. As long as you're willing to put forth the effort, a mini-tub kit is the only way to fit big tires under the rear of a muscle car.

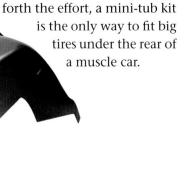

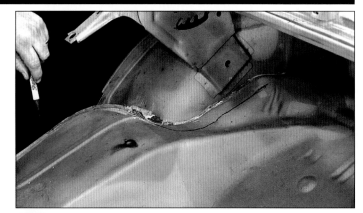

1 *Before doing any cutting or grinding, you should start by marking the desired cuts. Detroit Speed suggests making a mark 2¾ inches inboard of the tub. Some trimming is necessary to get a perfect fit around the curved transition areas.*

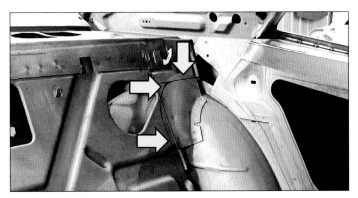

2 The rear seat panel must be cut using the marks seen here. Then, the spot-welds are drilled out, and the piece can be placed to the side until the new tubs are installed. The rear seat panel will be sectioned and re-installed when the new tubs are welded into place.

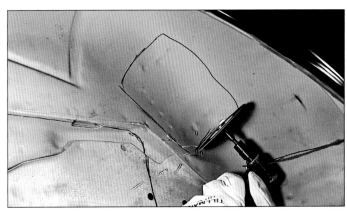

3 It's tough to cut out the wheel tub in one piece, so cut it into sections if necessary. Then you can trim the floorpan and trunk pan on the marks determined by the templates.

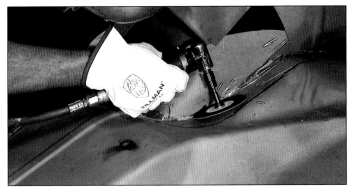

4 Most of the cutting can be performed with a pneumatic cut-off wheel. It doesn't offer a super-fast cut but you can be very precise, compared to the high speed of an electric grinder with a cut-off disc. Use a drill with a spot–weld cutting bit to make easy work of the original spot-welds on the rear seat panel and truck hinge bracket.

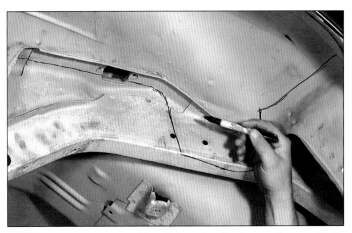

5 Now the underside of the wheel tub can be marked and prepared for cutting. The marks extend down into the rear frame rail. Detroit Speed provides templates for these panels and suggests using 1/8-inch steel plate.

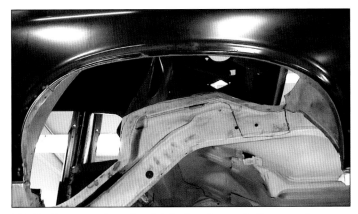

6 Remove the wheel tub, leaving only the rear frame rail notch to be cut and removed. A pneumatic cut-off wheel or plasma cutter can be used on the frame rail, which is slightly thicker steel than the wheel tub.

7 The new, deep tubs can now be test-fit to check for any clearance issues. This generally requires several tries to get the perfect fit. Additional trimming around the corners may be necessary for a flush fit all the way around.

8 *Here are the rear frame rails with the new 1/8-inch plates (not included in the kit) tack-welded into place. These notches help gain more real estate, and the plates require moderate fabrication skills. The rear portion of the frame rail notch features a slight curve, which can be made without any special metalworking tools.*

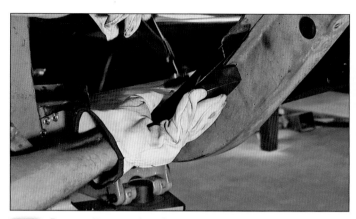

9 *Depending on the clearances, Detroit Speed suggests leaving a 1/2- to 3/4-inch strip of metal on the floorpan and trunk pan. These strips can be hammered over (using a dolly) to act as a mounting flange for the new tubs.*

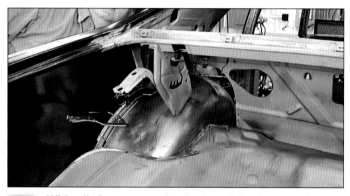

10 *With all clearances checked and the frame rails notched, you can clamp the wheel tub into place for the final time. Locking pliers (lots of them) are suggested, but you can also use sheet-metal screws or Cleco fasteners to secure the tub before welding.*

11 *Drill holes every 2 inches in the wheel-tub flanges, where they attach to the frame rail, floorpan, and trunk pan, but only drill through the wheel tub. Then, use a MIG welder to spot-weld the wheel tub to the car.*

12 *If you're building a leaf-spring car the following crossmember steps can be skipped, but if you're using a Detroit Speed QUADRALink rear suspension kit, you must install a new rear crossmember. After the necessary portion of the floor is removed, the "blank" crossmember is fitted and marked.*

13 *The crossmember can then be cut on the marks, which follow the bumps and contours of the floorpan. Use a cut-off wheel to make the cuts, and use a grinder to fine-tune the panel.*

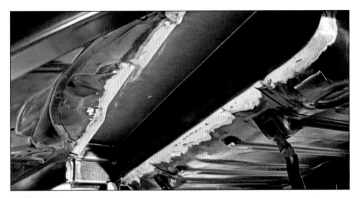

14 *After some tedious fitting, the rear crossmember can be welded into place. Welding this type of L-joint can be tough from the bottom side, so welding it from inside the car may be easier. Either way, sand the welds smooth with a grinder.*

15 *With the rear crossmember in place, the wheel tubs can be finish-welded. The rear crossmember serves two purposes: It strengthens the rear frame rails and raises the rear upper shock mounting points, leaving plenty of shock/spring travel when the car has a lowered ride height.*

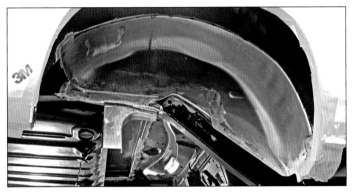

16 *Take your time when grinding the welds and you'll end up with a beautiful finished product like this. The plug welds are easy to grind without digging too deeply into the metal but any joint that is butt-welded (such as the frame rail filler plates) requires special attention, to prevent weakening the joint.*

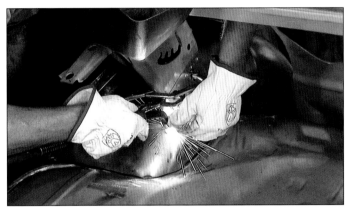

17 *Because the trunk hinge bracket usually mounts in the curve of the wheel tub, it must be sectioned to fit the new, wider tub properly. When you get it test-fitted, and everything checks out, the trunk hinge bracket can be spot-welded to the tub.*

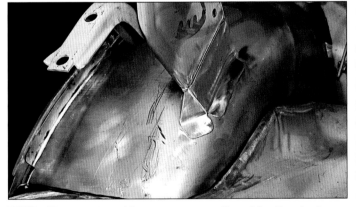

18 *Four spot-welds are now unnoticeable, thanks to a few minutes of careful grinding. Always be careful when assembling or disassembling trunk hinges because of the extreme tension on the spring.*

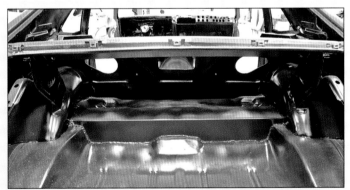

The finished product isn't alarmingly different from the original but it certainly provides a lot more real estate for wide tires and wheels. The rear crossmember allows for the QUADRALink but it also helps stiffen the rear portion of the chassis.

FRONT SUSPENSION

There is little doubt that a good first step for any Pro Touring project is a front suspension upgrade. Whether it's a bigger anti-roll bar, stiffer springs, or performance shocks, the front suspension is always a place to gain some ground in the handling department. It's common to see guys throw tons of money at front suspension and steering because it is truly the hardest-working part of the car in a road race or autocross environment.

With most muscle cars, the lack of front grip is equally as frustrating as the lack of rear grip. Although most folks think of muscle cars as "loose" cars (meaning the rear tires lose grip before the front tires), the truth is that the front suspension is the first place to start when trying to make an old car handle like a new one. Regardless of the budget or desired performance, front suspension provides many options for improvement.

The example used is a common platform in the Pro Touring world: a 1967–1969 Chevrolet Camaro. Although parts interchange does not apply to some of the other GM platforms (and obviously Ford and Mopar applications) it offers a general example of the positive effects of aftermarket front suspension components. The purpose of these components is to provide strength, reduce body roll, and increase traction. To accomplish this, a host of parts must work in conjunction to get the best possible result.

It also helps if particular components are adjustable, so you can dial them in to match your car's specific needs. For instance, a big-block car with 225/60R15 front tires may need different shock settings than an LS-swapped car with 245/45R17s on the front. Weight bias, tire size, and many other factors are involved in fine-tuning the suspension.

The first-generation Camaro had lots of great features that make it a staple from the muscle car era. These cars were in every high school parking lot in the United States for quite some time, and it's part of what makes them so popular now. Remembering those times in your Camaro often evokes memories of tire smoke, screaming engines, and maybe even an encounter with the local law enforcement.

We often forget the fact that these cars do not handle well in stock form. When muscle cars were new, the handling may have seemed adequate for the time but with our

Throughout this book, the build-up of this 1969 Camaro is followed, which rolled into Detroit Speed as a COPO clone. The plain-Jane look, combined with a big-block and 4-speed transmission, makes this a highly desirable car, but owner Mac Martin wanted a real performer.

Underneath, Mac's Camaro still had all of its stock equipment and had undergone a complete restoration. Turning this car into a Pro Touring machine would be a straight-forward process using the Detroit Speed catalog of parts for first-generation Camaros.

modern standards, hopping in a vintage Camaro provides quite disappointing results. The steering doesn't do what you want, the brakes don't do what you want, and you cringe when you pitch it into a corner too quickly, only to realize it just flat out doesn't stick to the pavement as it should.

Thankfully, all of these problems can be resolved without getting too deeply into the race car realm. Simple fixes generally reel in the bad handling characteristics, at least to the point of moderate street performance.

The beauty of GM unibody cars is the front subframe design, which completely unbolts from the car in one piece. Remove a few bolts and the entire subframe, engine, and transmission drop from the chassis. A new Detroit Speed hydroformed subframe will be bolted in its place.

Most muscle car guys would weep if they knew that a perfectly restored big-block Camaro was being dismantled in favor of a custom build. The beauty in all of this is that the subframe and engine could be stored and reused if the owner has a change of heart.

This is Detroit Speed's hydroformed subframe in its bare form. The subframe is resting on jack stands and the new engine and transmission are mocked up before the front suspension is assembled.

When the car reached completion, the Detroit Speed crew lowered the 1969 Camaro body over the new subframe and bolted it into place. Other modifications had already been performed, so this was one of the final steps to getting the car back on its feet.

However, once you are bitten by the autocross bug, you find yourself trying to reduce weight in every possible area, fooling with tire pressures, and buying high-end parts. One of the many great aspects of Detroit Speed components is the race-proven design. Whether you buy a single product, such as a control arm set, or a complete handling package, you get parts that truly work on the track and on the street. The bottom line is to change what the car manufacturers got wrong back in the day.

Repairing those original problems starts with modifying the car's front suspension geometry, an area with which Detroit Speed owners, Kyle and Stacy Tucker, are very familiar. Their background as GM engineers gave them the experience to make classic cars perform as well as new performance cars, without an incredible amount of effort from the consumer. The beauty of most muscle car front suspension parts is that you can bolt on new parts and hit the road with noticeable results. If you're an experienced gearhead with the appropriate tools, you can completely rebuild a front suspension system in a weekend, and dramatically change the car's attitude and performance.

Geometry 101

If you remember geometry from high school, it's time to put those lessons to good use. Suspension geometry can be a confusing subject but it's a very important part of making a vehicle handle and perform well. Caster, camber, and toe are the three basic forms of measurements in front suspension alignment but they also explain a great deal of the suspension's geometry. These measurements also point out the shortcomings of original independent front suspension systems from the 1960s and 1970s. Many other terms associated with suspension geometry, such as roll center, roll angle, and roll axis, dig deeper into the mysterious world of unequal-length A-arm suspension but let's just cover the basics here.

The finished product is an incredible example of taking a bone-stock muscle car and transforming it into the ultimate Pro Touring car. The visual effect is great; you can see exactly what the right stance and tire and wheel combination can do for a classic muscle car.

The front suspension on this car is set up for high-performance handling, and the wide footprint of the tires hints at this car's capabilities. It's a drastic change from when it rolled into the shop, and there's nothing stopping you from doing the same with your muscle car.

Camber

The term *camber* gets thrown around a lot in the automotive world because it's the easiest to identify with the naked, untrained eye. Most car guys can spot a car with aggressive negative or positive camber without even trying, so it tends to be the most popular topic when it comes to suspension alignment. Although it is

important, it is just one of three very crucial adjustments to consider.

If you're wondering about the exact definition of camber, here's a quick one: Camber is the angle of the tire's vertical plane when viewed from the front or rear of the vehicle. Did that help you figure it out? Don't worry if you're still scratching your head; a visual aid is always helpful when explaining suspension alignments, so some examples are illustrated to help put this into perspective.

If the suspension is aligned in a manner that results in the front tires being completely plumb or vertical at ride height, the camber alignment measures zero degrees. Negative camber means that the top of the tire and wheel is tipped toward the centerline of the car. Positive camber means just the opposite: The top of the tire and wheel is tipped away from the centerline. Even in OEM applications, camber is rarely set at exactly zero degrees, even though most cars appear to have a tire that stands straight up and down.

A great way to put this in perspective is to look at a NASCAR Sprint Cup car in action at an oval track, something you've probably seen a million times. Most of the time, these cars have what seem to be wacky camber angles. The left-side (driver's) front suspension features lots of positive camber, while the right side (passenger's) features negative camber. The positive-camber gain on the (loaded) right side, combined with the negative-camber gain on the (unloaded) left side, results in a level

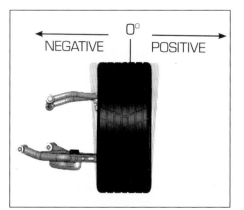

Camber is the easiest suspension term to grasp and it's very important to know how it affects the grip. Camber at ride height is easy to correct (with alignment shims) but to correct original camber geometry, you need aftermarket control arms. Be careful with cheap tubular arms because they may be built with original geometry specs. (Photo Courtesy Detroit Speed)

This photo of Kyle Tucker's second-generation Camaro illustrates the negative camber settings he uses to achieve maximum grip and forward bite through the corners. This sort of aggressive suspension tune is not necessary for most Pro Touring builds; it causes uneven tire wear and does not provide comfortable street driving.

contact patch, allowing the slicks to do their job. Those alignment settings are great for a car that makes only left turns, but what happens when you want to make left *and* right turns? You find a happy medium that keeps both front tires planted and gaining forward momentum.

In hardcore autocross and road race configurations, you can expect to see some noticeable negative camber adjustments. This is because of the positive camber gain on the outside front tire that occurs during hard cornering. As you gain positive camber through the corner, the loaded suspension levels out the camber angle, allowing the front tire to grip the surface using most of its contact patch. In most cases, the outside tire is doing all the work through the corner, and providing the bulk of the traction. That's the reasoning for negative camber on cars that have to make both left and right turns: It allows the outside tire (left or right) to be planted when the suspension is loaded.

Excessive negative camber is not ideal if you plan on driving your Pro Touring car thousands of miles to and from an event. It's rough on tires during regular driving conditions because the innermost portion of the tread is the contact point in straight-line cruising situations. Positive camber has the opposite effect on tire wear but there aren't many instances where positive camber settings should be on your radar.

Caster

Caster is a little harder to notice when the front wheels are pointed in a straight line, but you really notice a difference in caster settings when the wheels are turned in one direction or the other. Caster refers to the steering axis, which is an imaginary line between the centers of the upper and lower ball joint. The angle between the steering axis and the vertical plane (perpendicular to the ground) determines the caster angle. In other words, caster is considered zero degrees (also known as neutral) if the upper and lower ball joints are perfectly aligned when viewed from the side. You might assume that caster is set up neutral from the factory, but just like camber, it is a crucial part of the alignment process, regardless of the application.

Altering caster angles provides big improvements in suspension geometry and, ultimately, the handling of your vehicle. Caster adjustments are generally made with only the upper control arm; the lower control arm and ball joint remain in a fixed location. Positioning the upper ball joint farther to the rear of the car is considered positive caster, while positioning the upper ball joint farther to the front of the car is negative caster.

Most vehicles with independent front suspension are aligned using positive caster. This allows the vehicle to track straight and it improves the steering's "self-centering," while also providing a "heavier steering wheel feel" to keep the driver in touch with the location of his or her front tires and wheels.

Most upper control arms have very little adjustability in terms of caster because the cross shafts do not allow for any major movement where the control arm attaches to the chassis. However, Detroit Speed offers a cool product called "Caster Tuners," which are oval-shaped inserts to fit in its tubular upper control arm cross shafts. The center-punched inserts are set up for stock caster settings, but Detroit Speed offers these in two more-aggressive settings, which offsets the mounting hole of the upper control arm. This positions the upper ball joint farther to the rear of the vehicle, thus increasing positive caster.

The benefits of positive caster are far beyond simply making the car handle well under regular street driving conditions. Positive caster adjustments also allow the outside (loaded) tire to gain negative camber, yet another step in planting the front tires and getting optimal traction through the corner. Positive caster also helps with bumpsteer.

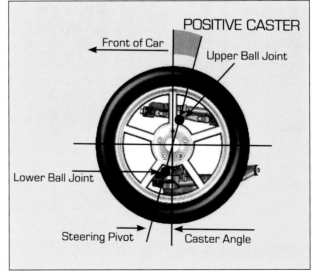

Caster is a little trickier, but this illustration provides a look at a positive caster setup. The upper ball joint is positioned farther toward the rear of the car than the lower ball joint. Caster geometry is the biggest downfall of stock front suspension setups. (Photo Courtesy Detroit Speed)

Toe

Toe adjustments refer to the alignment of the front tires from a bird's-eye view, looking down on the front suspension from directly above. If the tires are pointed toward the centerline of the vehicle (toward each other), it is considered "toe-in" and if the tires are pointed away from the centerline of the vehicle (away from each other), it is considered "toe-out." Just like caster and camber, OEM alignment specs might appear to be completely neutral (zero degrees) even though most auto manufacturers specify a certain amount of toe to ensure comfortable and safe driving characteristics.

In most cases (especially in rear-wheel-drive formats), toe-in adjustments reduce oversteer while also steadying the car at high speeds. Obviously there's a limit to the amount of toe-in you can adjust into the front suspension, as the scrub effect of the tires comes into play even with as little as 1/16 inch of toe-in. With the tires working against each other, an aggressive toe adjustment can shorten the life of the front tires dramatically and provide some odd tread wear patterns. On a rear-wheel-drive vehicle, toe-out adjustments are rarely used because of instability issues.

Although most Pro Touring builds spend more time on the street than on the racetrack, the folks who go all-out certainly toy with each form of suspension geometry to find the right combination for their machine. It's part of the process that means just as much as the aftermarket components that you choose to install. You can get a truckload of fancy suspension components, but if you're not taking advantage of better suspension and steering geometry, the results are not ideal.

Ride Height

Before I get into individual parts of the front suspension of most muscle cars, I'll address the first question that most people have, and that is ride height. Muscle cars stood tall from the factory, so it's pretty common for folks to lower the ride height, even if they don't plan to go fast and corner hard. Just like any other automotive modification, there is a right way and a wrong way to lower the front suspension. First of all, put the torch away; you do not need it.

Using a torch to heat the coil spring to the point of collapsing is the absolute wrong way to lower a car. Sure, it lowers the car, and you can do it without turning a single wrench, but it's just downright dangerous. It weakens the coil spring, which ruins any car's handling abilities. Fortunately, there is another cheap, at-home solution to lowering the ride height that actually works. Cutting the coil springs is an accepted way to lower a car because, in most cases, it increases the spring rate. This stiffens the front suspension, helping to resist body roll under hard-cornering situations.

To perform this modification you must remove the springs, and use a cut-off wheel (or any metal-cutting device) to remove a portion of the coil spring. It's common to see enthusiasts cut a "round" out of the springs, which means removing the first full coil in the spring. This usually equates to about 3 inches, but it varies based on the make and model of your car or truck.

The most desirable way to lower the front suspension on a car from the muscle car era is to use a pair of drop coil springs. Many options are available for various ride heights and spring rates, allowing you to perfectly dial in the stance and handling performance.

The absolute worst way to lower the front suspension is by heating the coil springs with a torch. Sure, this makes quick work of putting your car in the weeds, but it completely ruins the springs by taking the tension out of the metal. As you can see, excessive heat has collapsed this coil spring.

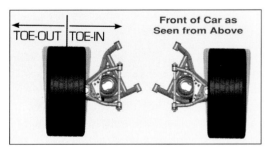

Toe *is an important part of front suspension geometry and it's one of the easiest parts to adjust. Generally, toe adjustments are minor, so as not to create unnecessary resistance between the front tires and the pavement. (Photo Courtesy Detroit Speed)*

With the coil springs out of the car, you can see that they were no longer doing their job as intended. Heated springs create a very spongy ride characteristic, which obviously isn't ideal for hard cornering. Lowering springs is the correct way to lower the front suspension without sacrificing ride quality or performance.

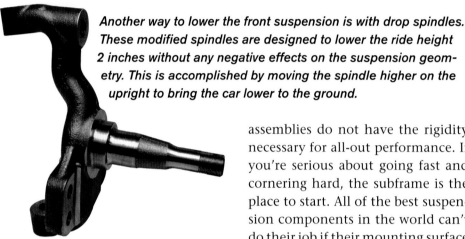

Another way to lower the front suspension is with drop spindles. These modified spindles are designed to lower the ride height 2 inches without any negative effects on the suspension geometry. This is accomplished by moving the spindle higher on the upright to bring the car lower to the ground.

Another great method involves swapping to a drop spindle. These aftermarket spindles lower the suspension without messing with the suspension alignment, although some aftermarket spindles feature a different overall height to help with suspension geometry. Using a drop spindle with an original coil spring doesn't improve handling, because of poor spring rates and metal fatigue.

Drop springs and drop spindles are affordable options that work well on mildly modified Pro Touring builds. High-end builds generally feature an aluminum-bodied coil-over shock design, which provides vast adjustability.

Subframe and Front Suspension Assembly

It may not seem like a weak point but original GM subframe assemblies do not have the rigidity necessary for all-out performance. If you're serious about going fast and cornering hard, the subframe is the place to start. All of the best suspension components in the world can't do their job if their mounting surface isn't strong enough for the abuse. In addition, the 40-plus-year-old subframe under most GM applications has lost a lot of its strength after years of use. Factors such as metal fatigue, rust, and accidents can cause the subframe to lose its ability to withstand the rigors of aggressive driving, so Detroit Speed developed a solution that surpasses the original unit by leaps and bounds.

Originally, automotive manufacturers used various methods to produce frame rails. Most methods involved stamping two pieces of steel into a C shape, and then welding them together to create a box. Although this served the purpose when muscle cars were in their infancy, the design is susceptible to flexing, which is the enemy of a Pro Touring car. It was not until the late 1990s that General Motors began using hydroformed frame rails on the revolutionary C5 Corvette.

Guess who was on the chassis development and analysis team

The original front subframe isn't likely to be rusted out or worn beyond repair but it is likely to be tweaked from years of abuse. Aftermarket subframes take all the guesswork out of it, and provide a blank canvas to build upon.

Good, Better, Best Comparison

So, you want the car to handle well but you're not sure if you need the full-tilt setup that might also be used on a high-end Pro Touring build. Front suspension is a great place to experiment with various components to find the right mixture for your vehicle. You may not need double-adjustable coil-overs with rack-and-pinion steering if your build is a casual driver. With this in mind, let's take a look at three different levels of upgrades to the front suspension on a GM F-Body platform (1967–1969 Chevrolet Camaro and 1967–1969 Pontiac Firebird).

Good

If you're going to do a piecemeal suspension build, this is the first group of components to buy and install. New bushings and ball joints are a must for any build, as are the steering rebuild components. A large-diameter anti-roll bar helps stabilize the suspension, while adjustable shocks and lowering springs help control the suspension actions.

Component	Price
New replacement control-arm bushings	$55–150
New replacement ball joints	$35
Adjustable Koni shocks (pair)	$270
1⅛-inch anti-roll bar	$210
New 2-inch lowering coil springs	$195
Stock-style steering service kit	$315
Price of base upgrades	$1,080–$1,175

Better

The next step is to upgrade the suspension geometry with a set of Detroit Speed tubular control arms. The arms make a huge difference in handling, especially when combined with a coil-over conversion kit. Detroit Speed tunes the shocks, and offers a choice of 550- or 650-pound-per-inch spring rates. At this point, you will also upgrade the original steering gearbox and power assist unit. Even though the 600 gearbox is much better than stock, the steering system still leaves a bit to be desired compared to rack-and-pinion.

Take "Good" ($1,080-$1,175) and add these parts:

Component	Price
Detroit Speed tubular control arms (upper)	$695
Detroit Speed tubular control arms (lower)	$675
Detroit Speed coil-over conversion bracket	$400
Coil-over shocks (pair)	$500
Coil-over springs (pair)	$138
600 steering gear (base price)	$595
Power steering pump (base price)	$175
Price plus base upgrades	$4,258–$4,353

Best

If you're serious about Pro Touring, it makes the most sense to skip the "Good" and "Better" steps and go all-in with the Detroit Speed hydroformed subframe assembly. This is the complete package, ready to bolt onto your car and hit the road. It comes preassembled and every component is top-shelf equipment for a Pro Touring build. Although the pricing may be intimidating ($7,000 base price), the proven results and easy installation make this a no-brainer for many Pro Touring enthusiasts.

The features include:

- New hydroformed frame rails with stamped crossmembers
- Detroit Speed tubular control arms
- Coil-over shocks with "Detroit Tuned" valving for your combination
- Coil-over springs with specific rate for your combination
- Power rack-and-pinion steering
- Splined anti-roll bar
- Forged steering knuckles (spindles) ∎

during that period? If you answered Kyle Tucker, you'd be correct.

Kyle took what he learned with the C5 Corvette and applied it to the subframe that rides beneath the 1967–1969 Camaro, 1970–1981 Camaro, and 1968–1974 Nova platforms. He knew that hydroforming the steel frame rails creates the strongest core, so Detroit Speed designed a bolt-in subframe that provides a strong base for high-performance suspension parts. The seamless frame rails are formed at low temperatures, unlike in traditional manufacturing processes, which do not preserve the steel's strength. The main advantage here is strength and rigidity, but it

Detroit Speed's hydroformed subframe offers a much stronger platform, and it's the perfect backbone for a full-on Pro Touring build. Even if you have the best suspension components on the market, the subframe has to be rigid enough to take the abuse.

The 1962–1967 Chevy II had a very simple subframe design but it's not quite as strong as the Camaro's. This is due to the mounting location and the fact that the Camaro subframe extends beneath the car, whereas the Chevy II subframe bolts into place at the firewall.

also allows Detroit Speed to repeat this process with great precision.

The crossmembers in Detroit Speed's hydroformed subframes are stamped and welded into place, as are the control-arm mounting points. The main engine crossmember is patterned on the original GM piece, so bolting in a small-block, big-block, or LSX engine is just a matter of bolting up the appropriate mounts. The Detroit Speed subframe also accepts Pontiac engines for the Firebird and Trans Am. If you want to keep the mechanical clutch linkage, Detroit Speed offers an optional Z-bar bracket.

Another big advantage of the subframe is its provisions for rack-and-pinion steering to replace the sloppy gearbox that General Motors installed in the 1960s and 1970s. Detroit Speed also builds these subframe assemblies to accept a splined anti-roll bar and coil-overs, a huge step ahead of the stock equipment. The fact that the subframe comes fully loaded with Detroit Speed's front suspension makes the subframe assemblies an easy bolt-on addition to any hardcore Pro Touring build.

Control Arms

More than any other component in the front suspension, the control arms are responsible for most of the geometrical problems that plague muscle car handling capabilities. Caster and camber play a huge role in a car's performance, and the stock control arms cannot provide the optimal adjustments necessary. In addition to the terrible handling characteristics, the original arms are made from stamped steel, which isn't strong enough for serious abuse. Original control arms suffer from deflection under harsh driving conditions, and that's only the beginning of a long list of disadvantages.

Tubular control arms have been on the market for quite some time but it's important to know that the ones you can buy on eBay for $200 are not designed for performance. Generally, the cheap control arms

are copied from a popular design and you get what you pay for in those instances: Poor metal and weld quality make for a lackluster product. If you're buying control arms because they look cooler than the original stamped-steel units, the eBay arms are suitable, but you're still buying them for the wrong reason. Be safe; don't buy knock-off control arms.

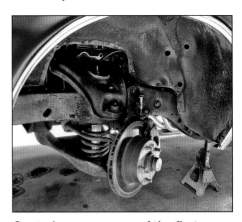

Control arms are one of the first things you should consider on your list of suspension modifications. The original steel stampings are flimsy and have very poor geometry. Installing new control arms is simple and effective.

Improving camber gain throughout the suspension cycle is the biggest advantage to a quality set of control arms. Most independent front suspensions do not allow the front tires to grip effectively because of poor suspension geometry. To put that into motion, a car making a right-hand corner throws all of its weight to the left side, which puts the stress on the left front tire. As the suspension leans and flexes, the left-side suspension suffers from positive camber while the right side is unloaded, causing negative camber.

Front Suspension Assembly for Mustangs

Although this book concentrates mostly on Camaro, Chevy II, Nova, and Chevelle platforms, it's important to note the reason for the heavy GM influence. Supply and demand play into the popularity of these GM builds; furthermore, limited front suspension options previously hindered efforts to build an early Mustang into a Pro Touring car. In response, Detroit Speed has introduced the Aluma-Frame, which is a front suspension module designed to fit 1964–1970 Ford Mustangs. It's a bolt-in unit that provides provisions for a highly functional Detroit Speed front suspension setup.

Originally, Mustangs were configured in a manner that attaches the spring and shock on top of the upper control arm, compared to most suspension systems, which mount the coil and shock to the lower control arm. This detail is what necessitates the bulky shock towers seen on most 1960s Fords. Detroit Speed's Aluma-Frame front suspension setup replaces the entire front suspension assembly with a brand-new setup. Instead of modifying control-arm mounts, spring location, and anti-roll bar configurations, this frame unit bolts into place and has all of the improvements built in.

The frame components (the cradle) are made of cast aluminum and bolt into place using Grade-8 fasteners. The original front frame rails are sandwiched between the two portions of the cradle. The upper portion features mounts for the upper control arms, as well as the coil-overs. The lower portion features mounts for the lower control arms, anti-roll bar, and rack-and-pinion steering system.

The lower portion of the cradle can be configured to accept many types of engines, from the basic small-block Ford to mod motors and even GM LS engines. Detroit Speed also offers a shock tower delete kit, which includes stamped pieces of 18-gauge sheet metal used to replace the bulky shock towers and provide sufficient engine bay clearance.

The Aluma-Frame system is a welcome option for Ford guys wanting to enter the Pro Touring world. Detroit Speed built these components, along with a number of rear suspension components, and tested them on the beautiful 1966 Mustang Fastback that is featured in Chapter 10. ∎

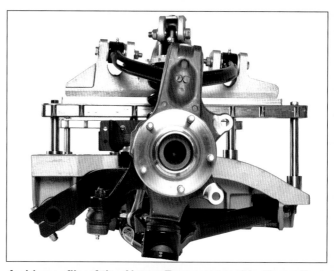

The Detroit Speed Aluma-Frame assembly is bolted together to illustrate how it mounts to the original Mustang front frame rails. The aluminum cradles offer superb strength without weighing down the front of the car. The Aluma-Frame is a complete package, with control arms, rack and pinion, coil-overs, anti-roll bar, and spindles. (Photo Courtesy Detroit Speed)

A side profile of the Aluma-Frame assembly shows its compact design, which offers lots of options for engine fitment, as well as more room for tire and wheel fitment. The aluminum cradles bolt to the frame rails using Grade-8 hardware. (Photo Courtesy Detroit Speed)

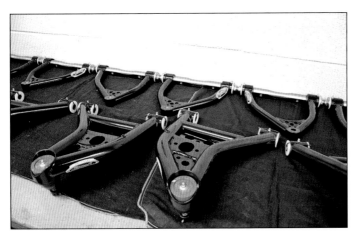

Detroit Speed's control arms are designed to give the front suspension additional positive caster and improved camber gain, which is very important in making an old dinosaur handle like a new Corvette. The arms are built in-house and come with a special Delrin bushing.

Ball joints and the end of the control arm take a lot of abuse, even in regular driving conditions, so it makes sense to get the best possible ball joints for your project. Moog ball joints are Detroit Speed's choice for all of its control arms.

Positive camber on the outside tire and negative camber on the inside tire is not the right combination; it causes a lack of grip, and that's obviously a bad thing. The term for a lack of front grip is *understeer*, when the front of the car tries to push through the turn.

The combination of poor suspension geometry, bushing deflection, and control arm deflection can cause some eye-opening handling issues. Ideally, you're going to drive hard into the corner, and with the appropriate control arm setup and suspension alignment, the grip from the tires is the determining factor of your success.

Detroit Speed's control arms increase camber gain and improve camber roll, while also incorporating caster tuner bushings into the stainless steel cross shafts. These bushings adjust caster by moving the upper control arm fore or aft for more or less caster without adding alignment shims. (I talk more about alignment later in this chapter.)

Detroit Speed's lower control arms are quite beneficial as well, offering improved geometry by increasing positive caster and lowering the coil-spring pocket. These arms feature a TIG-welded construction with gussets and a tubular cross brace for extra strength.

Many other aspects of the front suspension work in conjunction with the control arms but if you neglect the poor suspension geometry provided by stock control arms, the car will never perform as you want.

Bushings and Ball Joints

Bushings and ball joints are often neglected as key components in a properly working suspension because pretty much any restoration gets new bushings and ball joints throughout. Just like any other component in the front suspension, you can go back to stock if you so desire, or you can step up your game with heavy-duty parts

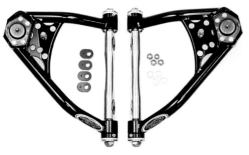

These are Detroit Speed's tubular upper control arms. They are designed to give the front suspension more positive caster, and they feature special cam inserts to tweak the mounting location fore and aft. This feature fine-tunes the caster settings independent of the camber settings.

A control arm install is one of the easiest tasks when it comes to building a Pro Touring car. The arms already have the cross shafts and bushings installed; all you have to do is bolt them to their original mounts.

Detroit Speed makes its own control-arm bushings using Delrin. This thermoplastic material is super strong, and it's perfectly reliable for the street. Detroit Speed mills a spiral groove in each bushing to provide a track for grease to travel.

The steel sleeves are also an important part of the bushing assembly. These are milled to perfection in Detroit Speed's shop before being sent out for plating. The Delrin bushing rides between the sleeve and the liner.

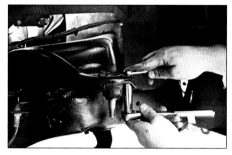

Even if you're retaining the stock control arms, a front suspension rebuild is not complete without a new set of ball joints. On GM cars, the uppers were originally riveted to the control arm and the lowers were pressed into place. New upper ball joints are bolt-in units.

that help the suspension assembly work in harmony. Control-arm bushings are very important in a vehicle's handling, so choose carefully among the many types.

Bushings with aluminum housings are available, but I suggest that you use a bushing with a steel housing because they allow you to spot-weld the housing to the control arm. This is especially important if you're using original control arms where the bore can be distorted from years of wear and tear. After the bushings are pressed into place, a few spot-welds can give you a little more assurance.

Rubber was the original material of choice for bushings, and it remains the best choice for a mostly stock muscle car. It provides plenty of give to help soak up the bumps, but that softness also hinders a vehicle's handling performance. Furthermore, rubber deteriorates quickly, becoming even softer until it eventually falls apart and creates a whole new set of problems.

It is common to use urethane bushings in a high-performance build but the best choice is a material known as Delrin. It is a thermoplas-

tic material that is very strong and resists wear. This bushing material is also very rigid to help keep the entire suspension assembly tight.

As for ball joints, they have one of the toughest jobs in the front suspension. They are constantly working, and that means that if you're tearing into the suspension, you need to replace the ball joints.

A high-quality replacement ball joint, such as a Moog unit, is perfectly sufficient, even for a high-end Pro Touring build. Moog ball joints are race-proven by NASCAR teams, and they are 100-percent endorsed by Kyle Tucker and the Detroit Speed crew.

Spindles

Another very important factor that is often overlooked is the spindles. Even gearheads look at an aftermarket spindle and wonder how it makes a real difference in handling. The truth is that most aftermarket spindles are not designed to improve handling; instead, they are designed to lower the vehicle by relocating the spindle on the upright. Although this is a perfectly acceptable way to

lower a car's ride height, the real handling differences come when the spindle works with the control arms to change the original geometry.

You might think the spindle's only job is to turn the front wheels and connect the upper control arm to the lower control arm. In reality, the spindle plays a much larger role in geometry because the total distance from the upper ball joint to the lower ball joint can greatly affect a car's handling. Changing this distance

Detroit Speed developed its F-Body front suspension to utilize a late-model Corvette spindle because it offered the correct geometry. Now Detroit Speed is building its own aluminum spindles to take advantage of more weight savings and a proprietary design. This component is one of the exclusive parts included in the Detroit Speed hydroformed subframe assembly.

alters the all-important camber curve and creates a totally different axis point for the suspension cycle.

Detroit Speed kits originally used a Corvette C6 spindle, which offered the correct geometry for its suspension systems. The forged aluminum design provides strength and weight savings over the original steel units, and proven performance is the key to including it in Detroit Speed's arsenal of race-bred suspension components. The C6 spindles already include provisions for huge disc brakes; Detroit Speed outfits them with custom forged steel steering arms to make the connection from the spindle to the tie-rod ends. A proprietary U.S.–forged aluminum spindle is now in production by Detroit Speed.

Springs and Shocks

In terms of working components in a high-tech Pro Touring suspension, springs and shocks rank highly on the priority list. Spring rates and shock valving is laughable in most stock muscle car platforms. The goal is to eliminate the slop and tighten the suspension to correspond with the weight of the car. To get it dialed in precisely, you need to know the weight and weight bias of your car.

When you read about suspension modifications and see that the goal is to make the car stay flat in the corners, you might think that stiffer is better. In most cases, that is somewhat true, but if the spring is too stiff and the valving is too tight, the suspension cannot do its job. That's where fine-tuning is involved, especially if you're dealing with slinging around the extra weight of a big-block.

The beauty of most high-end Pro Touring cars is that they have

been fitted with coil-over shocks. That means instead of having a coil spring and a shock absorber acting as two separate functions, you have an aluminum-bodied shock with a spring attached to it. Coil-overs require a bit of fabrication to mount them properly, but the result is certainly worth the effort. When installed properly, you can easily change ride height, spring rate, and shock valving without completely tearing down the suspension.

Most coil-overs come in single-adjustable and double-adjustable configurations, and a wide variety of springs are available to get the perfect match for specific applications.

Although all this hype about coil-overs is completely accurate for a serious Pro Touring machine, it doesn't mean you can't create a package that handles well with a set of simple springs and high-performance shocks. Again, spring rates are involved in choosing the right combination, but it's a cheaper and easier alternative than a coil-over

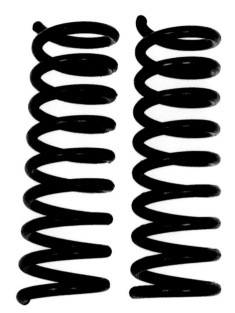

Various spring rates are available, and many springs are available to lower the car's ride height. There is no standard spring rate for muscle cars; every car has a different weight bias, which changes the desired spring rate. On most first-generation F-Body platforms, a small-block or LS-powered car needs a 550-pound-per-inch front coil spring; a big-block car uses a 650-pound-per-inch spring.

Swapping springs is an easy task that can be performed with simple tools and a floor jack. Be sure to place the jack underneath the lower control arm when you break the ball joint loose. This controls the tension in the compressed spring and allows you to easily take the pressure off the spring. Be extremely cautious: The coil spring has a lot of pressure on it.

Single-piece anti-roll bars are common for muscle cars but a splined anti-roll bar is the desired configuration. This design is used on road race cars and even NASCAR race cars, so it's race proven to keep the car level in the corners. Detroit Speed subframes are equipped with a splined anti-roll bar.

Coil-over shocks are very common in the Pro Touring world. Installing them to a stock front suspension requires welding new upper shock mounts into place but it's certainly worth the effort. Detroit Speed's tubular lower control arms are available with either standard spring pockets or provisions for coil-over shocks.

Although regular coil springs and shock absorbers are sufficient for a mild Pro Touring build, a set of coil-overs is a must-have for a serious corner-carving muscle car. Ride height and spring tension can be adjusted with the threaded body, and shock settings can be fine-tuned as well.

Anti-Roll Bar

Pretty much any car built during the muscle car era had an anti-roll bar on the front, and some had an optional bar on the rear. This bar is also known as a stabilizer bar or a sway bar. Without an anti-roll bar, any midsize (and especially full-size) passenger car throws its weight around with only the springs and shocks controlling body roll. This obviously isn't ideal for handling, so front and rear anti-roll bars are a must for any Pro Touring build.

conversion. Regardless of the decision, a bit of planning goes a long way in finding the perfect setup for the front suspension.

If you're building an all-out Pro Touring machine, you'll probably choose coil-overs, and you'll likely choose a shock that features a remote canister. This design incorporates a gas-charged bladder to provide high-frequency and low-speed dampening control.

One of the greatest contributors to a good suspension system is an appropriately sized anti-roll bar. Even if you're opting for a simple Pro Touring build, an anti-roll bar should be number one on your parts list. Be sure to choose a tubular anti-roll bar; it saves lots of weight compared to solid stock bars.

Bigger is usually better in the case of anti-roll bars; it's not uncommon to see folks use a 1⅛–inch bar up front and a 1-inch bar out back. Originally, anti-roll bars were solid pieces of steel, and most aftermarket units are built from thick-wall tubing to save weight.

Just as with any other aspect of the front suspension, the anti-roll bar can be a simple, bolt-on install for entry-level builds, or it can require some fabrication if you plan to run a race-inspired splined anti-roll bar, such as the one available on the Detroit Speed hydroformed subframe assembly. Regardless of your choice, a new anti-roll bar, bushings, and end links are a sure-fire way to make a sloppy muscle car feel a bit tighter in the corners. It obviously cannot take the place of a good set of springs and shocks but it certainly helps your car get through the corner.

Steering

Your car's steering system is an extremely important factor in its

Although many hardcore Pro Touring enthusiasts make the swap to a rack-and-pinion steering setup, it may not be necessary for the setup. Common replacement parts, such as the Pitman arm, idler arm, tie-rods, and hardware, certainly take the slop out of a stock steering system.

handling performance, as well as in its regular driving characteristics. All cars from the muscle car era were equipped with a steering box, rather than today's rack-and-pinion setups. A good steering box can make a world of difference in your Pro Touring build, especially if it's based on any of the GM platforms. A simple bolt-on swap to a 600 steering gearbox to replace the common GM 800 box is the first step to improving the car's responsiveness and overall feel.

General Motors didn't change its steering box design for quite some time. They believed in consistency, which is an admirable trait but not when you're trying to carve corners in a sloppy Chevelle. The low-friction

gear design inside the 600 steering box provides increased steering feel, while precision rack-and-pinion valve technology makes the box a must-have for any Pro Touring build. The steering ratio is a quicker 12.7:1 and the 600 box is 6 pounds less than the more common 800 unit. You can still use the original-style power Pitman arm, so this is truly a bolt-on swap.

If you want to take it a step further and ditch the box altogether, you can always opt for a rack-and-pinion steering setup. Conversion kits are available for many muscle car applications and provide moderately simple installation. A rack-and-pinion is not only an effective way to steer your

When it comes to upgrading a car's steering system, the gearbox is a great place to start. Detroit Speed offers a 600-series steering box, which is a direct replacement for GM 800-series boxes from 1964 to 1992. It offers a quicker ratio, a low-friction gear design, and a 6-pound weight reduction.

This is the answer to most steering issues: a rack-and-pinion. It saves a lot of weight compared with the old box and linkage, and it's a more-efficient design. Rack-and-pinion systems can be retrofitted to some muscle car platforms without major fabrication but it's nearly impossible to achieve the correct geometry when using a stock subframe. If a stock subframe is in use, Detroit Speed does not advise a rack-and-pinion conversion.

vehicle, it also weighs considerably less than a standard steering box and all of the linkage associated with it.

Converting to rack-and-pinion can sometimes cause a bit of headache because the steering shaft may require some creative routing to get past the headers, engine mounts, and front crossmember. New steering shafts, steering couplers, and rag joints are readily available for this sort of conversion but Detroit Speed does not recommend a rack-and-pinion conversion for the first-generation F-Body platform or many other platforms. The placement for the rack-and-pinion (when using a stock subframe) is not in the correct position to provide a benefit over the original geometry.

A problem known as bumpsteer falls under the steering category, and it can occur with stock steering systems, modified systems, or even rack-and-pinion setups. The term *bumpsteer* means that the angle of the steering linkage does not perfectly align with the arc of the control arms. In other words, hitting a bump or pitching the car into a corner might cause the toe to be out of whack during the suspension cycle. This obviously isn't ideal when it comes to front grip, so decreasing bumpsteer at all costs is advised.

Bumpsteer can also be unsafe in regular driving conditions because the sporadic movements of the steering and suspension system can cause the car to dart on a rough road. Bumpsteer is not good in a street driving situation and it certainly isn't good on the autocross or road course. Be advised that the darting sensation can also be caused by poor shock valving (too much rebound) or a suspension alignment with too much toe-out.

Adding or removing shims between the upper control-arm cross shaft and the mounting point adjusts camber settings. On Detroit Speed tubular control arms, caster is adjusted with cam-style bolt inserts in the cross shafts. Different inserts are available to move the upper control arm forward or rearward to adjust caster.

To fix bumpsteer issues, you must make sure the steering angle matches the arc of the control arms. To accomplish this, taller or shorter tie-rod ends as well as tie-rod shims may be used to change the geometry of the steering linkage. It's important to note that going too tall on the tie-rod ends may cause wheel clearance issues.

Alignment

Caster, camber, and toe are the three basic forms of suspension alignment. In reality, there are plenty more terms in suspension geometry but I kept it simple and used common names, which also refer to suspension alignment specifications.

To build a Pro Touring machine that handles like a road race car, you won't be able to take the Camaro down to the local shop to have it aligned to OEM specs. That isn't going to work with aftermarket suspension components and more-aggressive

Toe adjustment is simple but it's easier for a professional shop to get it dialed in with precise measurements. The tie-rod end can be threaded in or out to adjust toe. If you plan on eyeballing this, also consider that toe adjustment affects the indexing of the steering wheel.

suspension geometry. If you want to get the most out of the handling package, you'll want some pretty specific alignment specs.

Race shops that are familiar with road racing and autocross cars can align the suspension to your specification, but don't be afraid to toy with the adjustments to see what works and what doesn't. The biggest drawback of aggressive suspension alignment specs is tire wear, as you'll likely have uneven tread wear if you use a race-tuned suspension alignment on the street for a long period of time.

All of these settings and adjustments have one common goal: increasing front grip. This helps the car keep forward momentum through the corner, which is not always an easy task with most muscle car platforms. Weight distribution isn't always ideal on a muscle car but alignment adjustments that take advantage of Pro Touring–style suspension components go a long way in helping your car stick in the corners.

Project: Subframe Assembly and Installation

This installation is performed on a Detroit Speed hydroformed subframe but the same process can be used on the stock subframe. Here, the subframe is ready for assembly. Detroit Speed subframes come assembled; this is an overview of how it all goes together.

1 Lower control arms are the first component to be bolted into place. The joy of using aftermarket control arms is that the bushings and ball joints are already installed. Push Grade-8 bolts through the holes, and attach a nut to each backside. Tighten them to 95 ft-lbs.

2 Upper control arms are next, and it's important to slide a few alignment shims into place as a baseline. Because precise fixtures are used in manufacturing the preassembled Detroit Speed hydroformed subframe, its alignment settings are pre-set.

3 Install the upper control arms' bolts and tighten to 75 ft-lbs of torque. The stainless steel cross shafts and upper control-arm bushings are already installed.

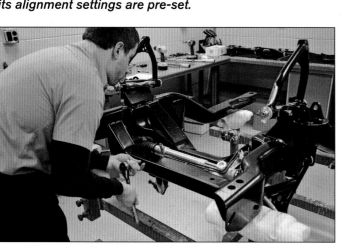

4 With the control arms bolted into place, the next step is installing the two long bolts to hold the rack-and-pinion in place, and tightening them to 95 ft-lbs. The Detroit Speed subframe features provisions for the rack-and-pinion system, whereas a stock frame is designed for a standard steering box setup.

5 Detroit Speed's splined anti-roll bar is based on a unique and advanced design that uses a bushing made of a special composite material to prevent noisy operation. A generous coating of grease during assembly provides a long life for the custom bushing.

6 Press the bushing into place to hold the splined bar. Install a retainer. During this time, make sure to center the bar, ensuring both sides are protruding the same amount. Be sure the bushings are fully seated during the measuring process.

7 Aiming the anti-roll bar arms in the twelve o'clock position is a great way to make sure both sides are even. Slide the arms into place and attach them with a single nut, which you tighten to 25 ft-lbs of torque. Do not install the anti-roll bar end links yet.

8 Now the coil-overs can be assembled. Each application uses a specific coil spring, and this one features a 550-pound-per-inch spring, which is advised for small-block and LS-based engines. Big-block cars usually require a 650-pound-per-inch spring.

9 A single bolt and nut attaches the top of the coil-over to the subframe. This is not possible with a stock subframe because coil-over brackets must be retrofitted. Torque the nut and bolt 70 ft-lbs.

10 *The bottom of the coil-over attaches to the lower control arm with two bolts and nuts, which you tighten to 35 ft-lbs of torque. This attachment point is not modified from the stock shock absorber mounting configuration.*

11 *Attach the anti-roll bar end links to the control arms and bolt them to the anti-roll arms. The first side attaches easily, and the second side should bolt together fairly easily, and without pre-loading the anti-roll bar.*

12 *Many of the bolts on the front suspension are torqued to the proper specifications but some are not designed to be super tight. Tighten the sway bar end links to 40 ft-lbs on the top nut and 45 ft-lbs on the bottom nut. A few drops of red Loctite keep the nut from backing off.*

13 *Now you can thread the tie-rod ends onto the rack-and-pinion. You can usually eyeball it to get the toe adjustment close, and then have an alignment shop dial it in.*

14 *The spindles can now be installed. On Detroit Speed's subframe assembly, mount the upper ball joint in the spindle and connect it through the control arm from the top. Tighten the retaining nuts and index them for the cotter pin.*

15 Use cotter pins on both ball joint nuts, as well as on the tie-rod nuts. Regardless of whether it's stock or modified, the front suspension requires these pins, and it's always a good idea to install new ones any time the suspension is assembled.

16 With the spindles bolted into place, the tie-rod ends can be attached to the spindles via Detroit Speed's forged steering arm. Torque the nuts to 60 ft-lbs and finish them off with a cotter pin.

At this point the front suspension is complete. It is best to wait for brake installation until the subframe is attached to the car. Other final details can be addressed when the car is sitting at ride height.

17 Installing a subframe assembly is usually a two-person job. It can be done with the body on jack stands and the subframe supported by a floor jack. Roll it into place and line up the bolt holes.

18 With someone operating the jack, you can line up the bolt holes and carefully adjust the subframe to fit. Detroit Speed also sells body mount bushings, which are suggested for any subframe installation.

REAR SUSPENSION

Now that you've learned how to make the front suspension keep the front tires planted, it's time to move to the rear of the car and find the problem areas. Although General Motors, Ford, and Mopar had various forms of front suspension styles throughout the muscle car era, they shared a common bond in many of their muscle car and pony car platforms. That common bond was leaf springs and a solid rear axle. It's an utterly simple design that leaves plenty of room for improvement,

which should make this chapter very educational, regardless of your brand preference.

Many GM midsize (A-Body) and full-size (B-Body) models featured a multi-link rear suspension with coil springs. I cover leaf-spring suspension as well as multi-link suspension in this chapter. Both are common forms of suspension in the Pro Touring world.

Leaf springs seem to be ancient technology if you look at automotive history. Because leaf springs

originated in the horse-and-buggy days, to say they are a bit archaic is a mighty understatement. The fact of the matter is that leaf springs can work in a Pro Touring environment with the correct setup that supports the car properly and keeps pinion angle in check at all times. Other options are available for converting your car to a multi-link rear suspension setup.

Many of the same goals of the front suspension are shared with the rear portion of the car. You want to reduce body roll and increase traction while lowering the car's center of gravity, and that requires aftermarket components. The confusion of suspension geometry is lessened by the simplicity of leaf springs, but a multi-link rear suspension brings geometry back into play by adjusting important factors such as instant center and anti-squat to increase rear grip.

Upgrading the rear of your Pro Touring build will likely involve more than just a few trick suspension parts. The rear-end housings in most GM applications were weak, and certainly not up to the task of a late-model high-horsepower engine. Even the strong housings

Oversteer is quite common for the high-horsepower cars that make up the Pro Touring hobby but it certainly isn't the fastest way around a corner. Although the driver probably has a huge grin on his face during this maneuver, it isn't ideal for going fast.

The rear suspension is a major weak point for many Pro Touring platforms, such as the GM F-Body, Ford Mustang, or any offering from the Chrysler Corporation. Whether you choose to do an upgraded leaf-spring setup or a custom multi-link rear suspension, modifications are necessary to build an efficient muscle car rear suspension.

Most muscle car and pony car platforms (aside from the GM A-, B-, and G-Body platforms) feature leaf-spring rear suspension. Leaf springs offer a stiff foundation but do not have any adjustability. Despite the limitations, the correct leaf-spring and shock combination can provide great low-budget performance.

that came from the Ford and Mopar camps had room for improvement internally; stronger differentials and axles are almost always desirable. A bulletproof rear-end setup can cost big-time money; but it's an important part of going fast.

There's no doubt that Pro Touring builds require a different approach to setting up the rear suspension than does a stock muscle car or drag racing–style car. A common misconception is that you want the rear suspension to be super stiff to reduce body roll. Although this is somewhat true, you don't want to take this too far because a stiff rear suspension may unintentionally turn your car into a drift car. Weight bias has a big effect on rear grip, but suspension setup can sometimes make up for a car that doesn't quite have the optimal bias of 50/50.

Let's dig a little deeper into what it takes to build an awesome rear suspension for your Pro Touring car.

Hardcore Pro Touring enthusiasts will likely opt for a multi-link rear suspension, as opposed to the stock leaf springs. This brings on a whole new level of adjustability, which is great for someone with the knowledge to make the most of it. The average car guy may not be ready for this sort of commitment.

Our example of converting a 1969 Camaro COPO clone into a Pro Touring beast offers a great perspective that crosses over to many other applications. Here, the car is sitting on its stock leaf springs, which use rubber bushings and mount to a stock 12-bolt rear end. This is not the ideal setup for a Pro Touring build.

The first step for the COPO transformation was to yank the rear end and leaf springs out of the car. Make note of the stock shock absorbers and drum brakes (even more equipment that is not conducive for a Pro Touring build). The rear-end housing can be reused but needs to be narrowed.

A number of auto manufacturers used leaf springs as a common rear suspension platform. Although leaf springs aren't the number-one choice, they are perfectly usable if you're not ready for a big suspension swap, such as the Detroit Speed QUADRALink, a four-link setup that fits in many muscle cars.

Leaf-Spring Suspension

If you're building a GM F-Body, X-Body, Chevy II, Mustang, Mopar, or even a classic pickup into a Pro Touring machine, listen up. As long as your car hasn't been cut up and

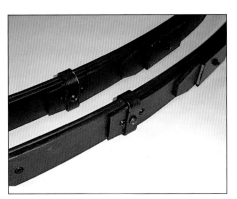

Some muscle cars came with a single leaf spring per side, whereas others featured a multi-leaf-spring pack. The multi-leaf pack offers more stiffness, and that is desirable in a Pro Touring configuration. Much as with the front suspension, determining the correct spring rate is a very important detail when it comes to setting up the rear suspension.

outfitted with a different style of suspension, you're more than likely dealing with a leaf-spring rear suspension setup, and that's not a bad thing. Before companies such as Detroit Speed began producing aftermarket multi-link rear suspension kits, most muscle car guys had to deal with leaf springs and learn how

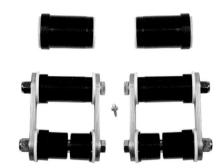

Shackles and bushings are important parts of a leaf-spring rear suspension. If you're planning to retain leaf springs, be sure to install new bushings. Delrin is the material of choice because it provides strength with great durability. New heavy-duty shackles also take some of the slop out of the suspension.

to make them work in a Pro Touring environment.

In most cases a 3,200-pound muscle car, such as a first-generation Camaro, needs a leaf spring with a spring rate of approximately 175 pounds per inch. Spring rates vary, based on each combination, but anything higher than 175 pounds per inch may result in poor ride quality. Rear springs that are too stiff also have the tendency to cause tire spin because of the lack of weight transfer. Aftermarket leaf springs are available for many applications, and in many cases you can also lower the ride height with custom springs.

To make a leaf-spring car work well in hard-cornering situations, you must also consider the leaf-spring bushings, shackles, and hardware. As with the front suspension, every working part of the rear suspension must be able to support the abuse. Rubber bushings are not always up to the task, so a set of polyurethane or Delrin leaf-spring bushings are recommended.

Detroit Speed recommends leaving the front rubber spring-eye bushing in almost all street cars with leaf springs. This is the "ride bushing," and using rubber allows just enough deflection to provide a comfortable ride. Using a solid urethane bushing in the front leaf-spring eye removes nearly all of the deflection but doesn't provide a comfortable ride. All Detroit Speed leaf springs are available with rubber front bushings and urethane rear shackle bushings.

Heavy-duty shackles are another way to take the slop out of the rear suspension, while new hardware, such as U-bolts and spring plates, helps keep a strong structure. Although leaf springs may be antiquated technology, you can make them work on a mild-mannered Pro Touring build.

Pinion Angle

When building a Pro Touring car using a leaf-spring rear suspension, it's important to dial in the pinion angle. In fact, pinion angle is an important aspect of any performance build. The term *pinion angle* refers to the angle of the driveshaft in relation to the pinion (where the rear of the driveshaft attaches). Lots of stress is placed on the rear-end housing during hard acceleration and deceleration, which causes the pinion angle to fluctuate a few degrees.

On a multi-link rear suspension, the length of the upper and lower link arms tunes the pinion angle, which is a fixed pinion angle. With a leaf-spring suspension, the pinion angle must be tuned with wedge-shaped shims that fit between the rear-end housing and springs, and the angle constantly changes due to the "wrap" effect of the leaf springs.

In most cases, you want the pinion angle to be negative (the rear of the driveshaft is slightly lower than the front) and the pinion pointed slightly toward the ground when the car is sitting still. The combination of these two angles creates the pinion angle. Drag racing applications may require as much as 7 degrees of negative pinion angle but Pro Touring applications may not need such an aggressive setup.

To measure pinion angle, it's best to use a magnetic angle finder. With the suspension at ride height, place the angle finder on the bottom of the driveshaft. Take note of the number (it's most important to note the difference from "zero," as this determines the driveshaft angle). Negative driveshaft angle is when the pinion end of the driveshaft is closer to the ground than the transmission end of the shaft. It's also important to note that negative pinion angle is when the pinion is pointed toward the ground. After determining the driveshaft angle, find the flattest area on the rear end (pinion flange is usually the best place) and measure the angle of the pinion.

As an example, if the driveshaft angle is negative 2 degrees and the pinion is at negative 2 degrees, it gives you a total of negative 4 degrees of pinion angle. In most cases, negative 4 degrees of total pinion angle is too much, so you need to adjust the upper control arms to rotate the rear-end housing. For a Pro Touring build using multi-link suspension, set the total pinion angle somewhere between negative 1 and negative 2 degrees (down). If using leaf springs, shoot for negative 4 to negative 5 degrees, to compensate for axle wrap

Pinion angle is important for any type of build but it's especially important on a leaf-spring car because of the rear end's tendency to twist under load. This condition is known as axle wrap, and it's not ideal in any situation.

For leaf-spring cars, wedge shims can be used to correct pinion angle, but a multi-link suspension can be adjusted by lengthening or shortening the control arms. Threaded arms provide plenty of wiggle room to get the pinion angle dialed in to your liking.

under acceleration. Pinion angle that is either too much or too little can result in driveline vibrations and premature U-joint failure.

Multi-Link Suspension

Despite leaf-spring rear suspensions being the most common platform in the muscle car era, it's hard to argue with the success of multi-link rear suspensions from the modern era. It's been proven time and again that leaf springs just don't provide the adjustability and flexibility of a good multi-link setup, so it's no wonder that multi-link setups are becoming commonplace in the Pro Touring market. In most cases a multi-link rear suspension must use a Panhard bar to resist side-to-side rear-end movement.

General Motors kicked off the multi-link rear suspension fad in 1964 when it introduced the A-Body platform chassis, to be used under popular muscle car models such as the Chevelle, GTO, and others. General Motors used multi-link suspension in its earlier B-Body (starting with the 1958 Impala) platform but the A-Body sparked the trend to make midsize cars handle like sports cars. There were many flaws in the original A-Body rear suspension design but it certainly provided a fresh outlook on rear suspension, compared to the parallel leaf springs that we had all come to know and love. There are major advantages to a modern multi-link rear suspension, and Detroit Speed perfected it with their patented swivel-link system, which is adaptable to many platforms, including those that originally featured leaf springs.

Multi-link rear suspension systems are much more complicated than the ancient leaf-spring design. However, with that complexity comes adjustability, which is the key to dialing in the handling on your Pro Touring beast. It all comes down to a perfect mixture of adjustments to get the most grip possible. There are many forms of multi-link rear suspensions, so let's take a look at the most popular types with a quick summary of pros and cons for each setup.

Two-Link

Generic rear suspension kits for many hot rods and street rods feature a two-link (ladder bar–style) suspension. This is perfectly suitable for a car that never sees any hard cornering, but a ladder bar leaves much to be desired in the world of rear suspension. The ladder bars provide one mounting point to the chassis and attach to the rear-end housing using two bolts per side. It's safe but not effective in the Pro Touring realm.

Another two-link option is known as a "truck-arm" rear suspension. NASCAR racers have used truck-arm suspensions for many years; the design was carried over from 1960s Chevy trucks, which had a two-link setup with extra-long control arms

Multi-link rear suspension is ideal for many reasons. It offers smooth articulation of the rear end without severe binding or the rebound that leaf springs produce. With Detroit Speed's QUADRALink, the adjustable control arms are threaded on both ends, offering lots of adjustability. Multi-link suspension conversions generally require welding and moderate fabrication skills.

When General Motors unveiled the A-Body platform in 1964 for its midsize platform, it featured a triangulated four-link setup with coil springs. General Motors borrowed this design from its B-Body platform but revised it for better handling and performance. With today's product availability, an A-Body car, such as this Chevelle, is a potent platform to build upon.

The two-link suspension is the most basic form of multi-link, and it's generally used in drag racing applications, such as the one pictured here. Most folks might dismiss this as a possible Pro Touring setup but NASCAR uses a two-link setup, commonly known as a "truck arm" suspension.

The torque arm rear suspension system is like an exaggerated three-link. It features two control arms and a long center link that extends forward to a particular mounting point. Third- and fourth-generation Camaros use this suspension and attach the torque arm to the transmission mount. The suspension pictured is an aftermarket system that features its own mounting bracket.

and coil springs. This setup is still popular with all-out road racers and oval-track guys because it provides decent articulation and a long "swing arm" effect on the rear end.

Three-Link

A three-link rear suspension features two lower control arms (like a regular four-link setup) and a single upper control arm that generally attaches to the center of the rear-end housing. The most common platform using a three-link rear suspension is the Ford Mustang, beginning in the 2005 model, and continuing on its most recent models.

The advantage of a three-link design is the elimination of "roll bind," a common condition with a triangulated four-link rear suspension. This seemingly endless amount of articulation is controlled with a Watt's linkage, which is a track locator, much like a Panhard bar.

Torque Arm

The third-generation Camaro may not get much love but it did bring a new style of suspension into the mix for General Motors. It was known as the torque arm, and it was a new take on multi-link rear suspension. The torque arm suspension featured two lower control arms and a single upper arm that ran from the rear-end housing to the transmission tailshaft housing. This design provides flexibility that leaf springs or a triangulated four-link cannot provide, and it provides a fixed instant center location, much like a two-link ladder-bar setup. The instant center is the (sometimes imaginary) point at which the upper control arms and lower control arms would meet.

On two-link and torque arm cars, the instant center location is generally the pivot point on the front links. Instant center locations (height and distance from the rear end) play a large role in how hard the car plants the tires. That means a parallel four-link car and a torque arm car feature very different traction capabilities, based on the instant center location.

The torque arm setup's long upper control arm eliminates axle wrap, so pinion angles stay very consistent. Moreover, although it was introduced in the third-generation F-Body platform, it is adaptable to earlier platforms.

Triangulated Four-Link

If you're dealing with a GM A- or B-Body platform, you're working with a triangulated four-link rear suspension. Another popular application with a triangulated four-link is the Ford Fox-Body platform used from the late 1970s to the early 1990s. The control arms are unequal lengths, and in most cases the lower arms are level and parallel with the frame rails. The upper control arms are triangulated, pointing toward the center of the rear-end housing, and they are shorter than the lower arms. The triangulated arms prevent lateral movement of the rear-end housing, thus eliminating the need for a Panhard bar.

This design provides a bit more flexibility than leaf springs but it does have a tendency to bind in hard-cornering situations. This "roll bind" condition is not a good thing, as you want the rear suspension to articulate freely when the springs are not attached. In other words, the spring should be the articulation-limiting factor, not the control arms. Although the GM A-Body platform leaves plenty of room for improvement, it provides a solid design that is easily modified with new control arms, springs, and shocks to completely revamp the handling capabilities and help with the poor geometry.

Parallel Four-Link

You may have heard of this type of suspension if you have been around hot rods or drag cars. This is a very common setup on the drag strip because it provides the most efficient design for straight-line performance. A parallel four-link suspension setup features four control arms that are the same length and parallel when viewed from the side and from the top. In combination with coil-over shocks, a parallel four-link setup

Parallel four-link setups have a few options: a four-bar, an equal-length four-link, and an unequal-length four-link. The four-bar (pictured) is a non-adjustable system, generally used for street rods. The equal-length four-link is often seen in the drag racing world, and the unequal-length four-link is used in the Pro Touring environment.

This photo illustrates a triangulated four-link suspension. The lower arms are generally in a straightforward position, while the upper arms are canted. On GM A-, B-, and G-Bodies, the upper links are mounted to the center of the rear-end housing. This configuration offers great flexibility but the Detroit Speed swivel-links increase it even further.

provides vast adjustability with multiple mounting points for the upper and lower bars. Moving the control arms affects the instant center, which controls the leverage on the rear-end housing and ultimately controls how hard the car launches. In a Pro Touring environment, a parallel four-link rear suspension can be used but the control arms must be adjusted differently than for a typical drag setup.

In contrast, some parallel four-link setups are designed specifically for road course use. Detroit Speed's QUADRALink is technically a parallel four-link design but it features unequal control arm lengths. The design is conducive to a straightforward installation, and it's obviously quite effective on the racetrack with proven results on many high-end Pro Touring cars.

Independent Rear Suspension

Even though most Pro Touring builds feature a solid rear axle, a few companies build aftermarket independent rear suspension systems. Independent rear axles are certainly cool but it's not the easiest way to keep the tires planted. In reality, there are a lot more "moving parts" on an independent rear suspension than on a solid axle, meaning more components to upgrade. With that said, there is no need to convert a solid axle car to independent.

Only a few American cars from the muscle car era featured an independent rear axle, the most prominent being the Corvette. It debuted the independent axle in 1963 and has kept it ever since. The first rendition featured a two-link trailing arm system with a transverse leaf spring and strut rods to tie it all together. The center section of the rear end is rubber-mounted to the chassis. A

This early Corvette independent rear suspension has very poor geometry that experiences drastic camber changes throughout the suspension cycle. A solid rear axle swap would actually be a major benefit to early Corvettes, but it's quite popular to retrofit these cars with modern Corvette (1984 to current) rear suspension and driveline components.

number of components are available to upgrade Corvette independent rear suspensions.

Rear-End Housing

Now that you've figured out the differences and options for rear suspension types, it's time to learn about the backbone of the rear suspension. Rear-end housings are not usually the weakest link in the assembly; it's generally the stuff that rides inside the housing that causes you the most trouble. However, it's pretty common to swap to a bigger housing for peace of mind and better

parts availability. Bigger isn't always better, though; excessive weight can become an issue to consider.

A common rear-end housing swap is based on the tried-and-true Ford 9-inch rear end. Although this rear end actually debuted in 1957, it still stands as one of the most common rear-end swaps. Its popularity is due to its strong internals and the removable carrier, which makes for easy gear swaps and rear-end maintenance. Just about every Ford vehicle from the 1950s to the late 1970s (Mustang, Galaxie, truck, etc.) had a rear-end housing with a removable carrier. They are plentiful and cheap to rebuild.

Most folks choose a Ford 9-inch housing because they're cheap and readily available. Ford introduced this rear end in 1957 and built millions of them, installing them in Mustangs, trucks, and anything else that might take a beating. Despite the great availability, a new housing is suggested to cut down on repair time.

However, just because it has a removable carrier doesn't mean it's a great rear end. Ford built a smaller rear end, known as the 8-inch, for many years, and it's not nearly as strong. You find 9-inch rear ends under some Mustangs, trucks, full-size cars, and more; the 8-inch rear ends are found under lesser-equipped Mustangs, Falcons, Mavericks, and so on. Despite the great capabilities, a 9-inch straight out of the junkyard may not be a bulletproof combination for your Pro Touring build, but a simple axle swap and a good limited-slip differential go a long way.

Another advantage of the 9-inch rear end is the ease of modification and repair. The axles are held in with bolt-on retainers on either side of the housing, and the carrier can be removed by taking out the 10 nuts that attach it to the housing. That means you can strip down a 9-inch rear end in a matter of minutes, which is especially handy if you have an extra carrier (with different gear ratios) ready to bolt in. Drag cars, Pro Touring cars, and regular street cars

put 9-inch rear ends to good use, but that doesn't mean that weaker rear ends aren't up to the task. With the right axles and differential, you can make any rear-end work with your combination.

General Motors introduced the 10-bolt rear end in 1964, moving away from its previous-style rear end, which featured a removable carrier (also known as a chunk, pumpkin, or third member). The first edition of the 10-bolt featured an 8.2-inch ring gear, and then an 8.5-inch version debuted a few years later. Eventually, a new, wimpy 7.5-inch rear end surfaced and gave the 10-bolt rear end a bad reputation. These rear ends generally rode beneath S-10 pickup trucks and many second-, third-, and fourth-generation Camaros and Trans Ams. You don't want a 7.5-inch 10-bolt; it's carnage waiting to happen.

General Motors introduced the 12-bolt rear end in 1965. This was a heavy-duty version of the new-style rear end, designed for heavier and higher-horsepower cars. It is a com-

mon swap in the muscle car world. The 12-bolt rear end features an 8.875-inch ring gear and 30-spline axles from the factory, but the weakest points are the axle retainers, or C-clips.

These clips are a drag racer's enemy, but you can also have issues with them during aggressive street driving if you're not careful. A rear end with C-clips is not advised in any car or truck that sees any type of abuse, whether it's drag racing, autocrossing, or spirited street driving. The C-clips hold the axle in place, and if a clip breaks, it means the entire axle can slide out of the differential. That means the tire, wheel, and axle can come out from under the car and cause major damage, not to mention the potential damage of sliding out of control due to the missing tire and wheel. If you plan on beating on your Pro Touring car but have a C-clip–style rear end, consider picking up a C-clip eliminator kit and save yourself a lot of trouble.

Mopar guys have a couple of good choices for rear ends. First is the trusty

Most of the big-dog GM muscle cars featured a 12-bolt rear end but you're most likely to see a 10-bolt beneath your project car. This rear end is an 8.5-inch 10-bolt. An easy way to tell if you have an 8.5 rear end is to look for the two triangular ears at the bottom of the center section.

The Chrysler Corporation had no issues with building a strong rear end. The 8¾ rear end is plenty strong, and the Dana 60 (pictured) is downright bulletproof. However, the strength comes at a price: excessive weight. You can outfit the rear ends with lightweight components to reduce weight, but at that point, it's simply a matter of preference.

8¾, which designates the size of the ring gear. As you can tell, the Ford 9-inch sets the benchmark; any ring gear that gets close to that size tends to be a popular choice. The 8¾ rear end is a great choice for midsize muscle cars because of the many options for differentials, gearsets, and axles.

The ultimate bulletproof Mopar axle is the Dana 60, which has a 9¾–inch ring gear. These monster rear ends were commonly used in high-powered muscle cars such as the Dodge Challenger, Plymouth Road Runner, and many more applications. The Dana 60 is readily available, but the biggest sacrifice of this indestructible rear end is weight: A stock Dana 60 weighs approximately 50 pounds more than an 8¾ rear end. But then again, I'm talking about stock versus stock. If you're going by the Pro Touring textbook, you save some weight by swapping to disc brakes, among many other weight-saving measures.

As you work your way through rear-end modifications, you may cringe at the thought of spending a couple thousand dollars just to make sure the rear end is up to the task. Yes, it's expensive, but it's also the smart thing to do. You can likely get by on a cheap rear-end setup if you don't plan to race your car on a regular basis, but you're leaving a lot on the table if you neglect the advantages of upgrading a stock rear end.

Gearing

Gearing is a crucial aspect of any performance car, whether it's set up for street driving, Pro Touring abuse, or drag racing. The final rear-end gear ratio affects drivability but it can also affect the way your car pulls out of the corners. Sometimes the gearing might provide the right "seat of the pants" feel but leave you searching for the appropriate (transmission) gear when you're on the autocross course. Many courses are set up for moderate speeds, so you're not likely to get any higher than third gear in most cases. So if the rear-end gear ratio causes you to constantly upshift and downshift to be in the power band, you're losing seconds with each shift.

As for overall gearing with regular street driving, there are many things to consider in finding what's right for your combination. Whether or not you have an overdrive transmission is a huge factor because you can generally get away with a lower ratio when you have that extra gear on the top end for interstate speed cruising. Too many RPM in high gear can result in the engine overheating, and it can also cause quite the annoyance if you have a loud exhaust system. Just about any engine sounds great when it's singing at a high RPM but that tune gets old after a six-hour road trip. Well, at least that's what your wife might say.

Part of selecting your rear-end gear is learning where the engine makes peak power. If you have a high-winding Ford Coyote engine, you might opt for a lower ratio (higher numerically) to keep the DOHC engine humming and make

You may never see the ring and pinion in your Pro Touring project car but it's important nonetheless. Strength isn't a huge concern but gear selection is the key to making your car respond the way you want. The engine's horsepower level and transmission selection play a huge role in selecting the rear-end ratio.

A high gear ratio (lower number, such as 2.73:1) provides sluggish initial acceleration but lets you reach a higher top speed. A low gear ratio (higher number, such as 4.11:1) gives you very quick acceleration but top speed is reduced dramatically. A low gear may also affect your car's drivability, unless you have an overdrive transmission.

the most of the efficient valvetrain design. On the other side of the coin, if you're using an old-school combination, such as a standard small-block Chevy, you want to keep cruising engine speed below 2,500 rpm to keep it happy.

Yet another aspect to consider is the transmission's first-gear ratio. Sometimes you select gear ratios based on starting-line acceleration, but many aftermarket overdrive transmissions feature a low first-gear ratio to help get the car up and going quickly.

Differential

You've selected the rear end and figured out the right gearing for your combination. What's next? The differential is another crucial piece of the puzzle, and there are lots of choices on the market. Stock differentials are not up to the task of Pro Touring abuse, and may even present some problems during regular street driving. The last thing you want is to drive into a corner and

The differential is a piece of automotive engineering that often gets overlooked. An open differential (pictured) features four spider gears that allow one rear wheel to spin faster than the other. A limited-slip differential uses clutches to apply torque to both rear wheels when necessary, and a locker is self-explanatory.

apply the throttle only to have the inside tire lose grip while the outside tire sticks. If you show off in front of your friends and only one tire spins you might be the punch line to many jokes and nicknames. Here are a few that you can use on your friends if this situation arises: Peg Leg, One-Tire-Fire, One-Wheel-Peel . . . should I keep going?

In the most basic terms, a differential helps your car get around corners. If both rear tires always rotated at the same speed, the car would bind up and chirp the tires as it makes its way around a corner. Drag cars that feature a spool or locker suffer from this problem but the totally locked-up differential is the ideal setup for straight-line performance. For Pro Touring, you want a differential that is much more versatile, allowing for optimal grip from both rear tires, without being too aggressive.

Clutch-style limited-slip differentials can be set up to perform on a Pro Touring car but the ideal setup is a gear-actuated differential, such as the Eaton Detroit Truetrac. This style of differential provides the straight-line performance of a locker, along with great cornering performance. It acts as an open differential during regular driving, but gear separation forces take effect and transfer torque to the high-traction tire at the moment of traction loss. The gear-style differential doesn't have wearable parts, and therefore doesn't burn up as a clutch-style unit does.

Axles

Although axles aren't nearly as important in a Pro Touring car as they are in a drag racing application, they still serve a great purpose. It's always advised to step

Axle strength is not extremely important in a Pro Touring application but you should note that all 10-bolt and 12-bolt rear ends feature C-clips to hold the axles in place. If an axle breaks, the remainder of the axle (still attached to the hub and wheel) can completely come out from under the car. You don't want that, so do yourself a favor and install a C-clip eliminator kit if you're dealing with a GM 10-bolt or 12-bolt, or a Ford 8.8 rear end.

up to at least a 31-spline axle and differential setup. Many stock rear ends (Ford, General Motors, or Mopar) come with 28-spline axles from the factory. These axles are not intended for performance use and often expire when horsepower and traction are combined. Even a mild-mannered street car can make waste of a stock 28-spline setup, so keep that in mind regardless of the type of rear end you choose.

Some Pro Touring enthusiasts choose to narrow their rear-end housing to fit wider wheels and tires. That's always an option, but it obviously requires new (shorter) axles, making it a good excuse to upgrade to a bigger and better set of axles. Again, you don't need the top-of-the-line 40-spline drag racing axles but a good set of axles gives you peace of mind.

Ride Height

Now that you've done your homework on the rear-end housing, and everything that lives inside it, you need to figure out where it should be located. A lowered ride height is always desired in a Pro Touring build because it lowers the car's center of gravity, offering stability and better handling characteristics. Lowering a muscle car is usually pretty simple but there are plenty of ways to do it wrong. Anything that involves a torch is just plain wrong; there are ways to affordably lower

your car's ride height without ruining its springs.

If your car features a coil-spring rear suspension, the always-popular method of shortening the springs usually doesn't work. Many coil-spring cars, such as GM A-Bodies, feature a coil that is drastically tapered on the top and bottom. This means that if you cut the coil to shorten it, you lose the tapered portion of the coil and the spring no longer fits into its perch correctly. The real solution is a new pair of springs. With new springs you can pick and choose the ride height, and you can also choose spring rate,

You can take a couple of different approaches to lowering the rear suspension. If it's a leaf-spring car, a set of lowering blocks is the cheapest and easiest route, but they do not offer any handling benefits. In fact, they add leverage to the rear end, increasing its tendency to twist under load.

which is a very important aspect of making the multi-link coil-spring rear suspension perform well.

For leaf-spring cars, you have choices. The most budget-friendly option is to use lowering blocks to space the rear-end housing away from the leaf springs. You can usually pick up a set of blocks for around $40 at the local parts store. It's an easy install and it's certainly effective at lowering the ride height.

However, lowering blocks do nothing to improve the car's handling, and actually hinder the car's performance by increasing the leverage of the rear-end housing against the leaf springs. This causes a condition known as axle wrap, meaning that when power is applied to the rear end, the housing rotates, which puts the leaf springs in a bind. When this happens, the leaf springs load and unload, causing less than desirable handling characteristics.

Control Arms

The rear control arms locate the rear-end housing and provide the path of motion through the suspension cycle. Control arms have many other names, such as trailing arms, links, and four-link bars. Keep in mind that when I mention control arm I'm referring to any link in a multi-link rear suspension.

Original multi-link rear suspensions featured a stamped-steel control arm, which allows deflection under a hard load. Many enthusiasts have boxed in the stock control arms with steel plate to make the arms stronger but that doesn't help with the poor geometry. In addition to the weak design, original-style control arms have been known to bind up as the suspension articulates. The

The correct way to lower a leaf-spring car is with a set of lowering leaf springs. These can be ordered in 2- or 3-inch drops, and they provide the stance you want without sacrificing ride quality or handling. Lowering springs are also available for multi-link suspensions. This 1968 Camaro features 2-inch lowering leaf springs.

Control arms are used in every form of multi-link rear suspension. Whether you have two, three, or four links, the goal is the same: smooth motion with no binding. A rubber or Delrin bushing is suggested for most street applications.

solution for this problem is a set of tubular control arms that provide strength and adjustability to the rear suspension system.

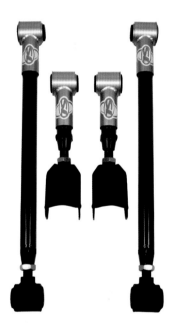

GM A- and G-Bodies have similar rear suspension setups and feature control arms such as these. The lower arms are long, while the uppers are short and mounted at opposing angles. This triangulated setup offers good articulation, but the Detroit Speed swivel-link control arms increase flexibility even more.

If you're swapping from leaf springs, a kit such as the Detroit Speed QUADRALink provides an easy solution for choosing control arms. The kit features an unequal-length four-link design with tubular upper and lower control arms fit with high-durometer rubber bushings. Why not urethane? In most cases, a urethane control-arm bushing is firm but also provides squeaky operation. The control arms are adjustable and feature Detroit Speed's patented "swivel-link" design, which allows the suspension to articulate with no binding. In combination with a pair of adjustable coil-over shocks, a Panhard bar, and an anti-roll bar, this rear suspension is light years ahead of leaf springs.

The length and mounting location of control arms play a huge part in rear suspension geometry, and also affect pinion angle. Thankfully, kits such as the QUADRALink system have the hard work figured out already. Some folks prefer to do their own geometry work to determine the correct control arm configuration but it certainly played into Detroit Speed's expertise to design a kit that is easy to install and really works on the track. The joy of the QUADRALink is that Detroit Speed makes it easy for you to weld in the appropriate brackets and control-arm pockets so that you can bolt the control arms into place and know that the rear suspension geometry is close to being spot on. Adjustability in the control arms allows you to tweak the setup to fit your Pro Touring machine.

Springs

Springs are important, whether they're on the front or rear, but the rear springs play the all-important role of keeping the rear tires planted in straight-line acceleration, as well as hard-cornering situations. Springs that are too soft make the rear suspension rely way too much on the anti-roll bar to keep it level in the corners. The bar is a supportive component of the spring, not the other way around. Rear springs that are too stiff result in a loss of traction because of a lack of weight transfer to the rear tires. For example, drift cars are set up with very stiff suspension so that the tires break loose at the hit of the throttle. On the other side of the coin, drag cars utilize a very soft spring to help transfer weight to the rear tires, thus increasing traction.

Finding the right springs for your Pro Touring build requires a bit of study but the weight of the car is usually the biggest factor. Because

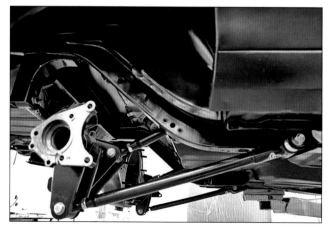

We follow along with a Detroit Speed QUADRALink rear suspension system, which replaces the original leaf springs with a multi-link suspension and coil-overs. The control arms are unequal lengths but feature a parallel orientation.

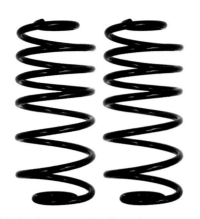

This is the type of coil spring you find under a GM A-Body. It features tapered coils on the top and bottom, so "cutting a coil" to lower the car's ride height is out of the question. Lowering springs are ideal, and give you the option to choose the spring rate to dial in the handling.

Regardless of your car's original suspension, a set of coil-over shocks is the right choice for most Pro Touring applications. You can still choose the spring rate, based on your car's weight bias, and then fine-tune the tension and ride height with the threaded aluminum body.

Mounting a set of coil-overs to your car requires welding and moderate fabrication skills. A crossmember must be welded to the car's floorpan, and mounting brackets must be welded to the rear-end housing. From there, it's simply a matter of bolting them into place.

spring rate is based on how many pounds of force it takes to compress the spring 1 inch, the car's weight is used to figure out the correct rate. A small, lightweight car, such as a Chevy II, may weigh less than 3,200 pounds including the driver, while a second-generation Camaro may weigh more than 3,400 pounds. Obviously, these two models require a different spring rate to achieve the desired handling. Finding the sweet spot isn't always easy for a hardcore Pro Touring car but a minor miscalculation (+/- 50 pounds) in spring rate isn't going to make a huge difference on the average street car.

It's important to note that leaf-spring rates should be less than 200 pounds per inch. A stock mono-leaf setup that rode beneath many Camaros and Chevy IIs features a spring rate of less than 100 pounds per inch; stock multi-pack leaf springs provide around 125 pounds per inch, and Detroit Speed's leaf-spring kits provide a spring rate of 175 pounds per inch. This is a vast

improvement to help stiffen the rear suspension. As for coil-overs, the desired rate can vary greatly depending on the car's weight, horsepower, and tire size (and compound). For most first-generation F-Body platforms, a 250-pound-per-inch rear coil-over spring is sufficient, but builds that generate more horsepower or carry a bit more weight require a stiffer spring.

Installing the springs is generally the simplest part of the entire process, especially if the car was originally designed with a multi-link coil-spring rear suspension. If you're using a kit, such as a Detroit Speed QUADRALink, you'll be installing a pair of coil-over shocks that feature an aluminum body and a steel coil spring. In this case, the most difficult aspect is welding the brackets to the rear-end housing, and welding a new crossmember to the rear portion of the chassis. From there, it's smooth sailing; the coil-overs simply bolt into place.

Coil springs are available in many spring rates, and they work in con-

junction with an adjustable shock absorber. Easy installation, easy adjustability, and undeniable performance make coil-overs a must-have for most Pro Touring machines. The coil-over shock assembly certainly simplifies Pro Touring builds.

Shocks

Rear shocks control a lot of movement in the rear suspension, and it's not a place to skimp, regardless of your choice of leaf springs or multi-link suspension. A good set of shocks can remove some of the violent rebound that leaf springs provide, and calm down the motion of the rear-end housing. Adjustable

If you're looking to do a mild upgrade to the suspension, a set of standard shocks, such as these Koni units, may be the best choice. Don't expect a shock absorber to carry the weight of the suspension; it is merely a dampener.

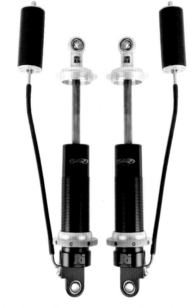

Hardcore Pro Touring and road race enthusiasts need a shock that can do some serious work and survive. These JRi shocks feature external reservoirs to hold additional fluid, which keeps the shock from overheating and, thus, losing performance.

offers pre-tuned shock absorbers for most muscle car applications. Detroit Speed also offers single-adjustable and double-adjustable JRi coil-over shock absorbers for all-out builds.

Adjustable shocks can also get you into trouble if you're unsure which direction to tune them. It can make a bad day at the track even worse but it's also a great learning experience for the novice Pro Touring enthusiast. Before you know it, you'll be bragging to your buddies about the shock package and throwing terms such as "valving," "jounce," and "rebound travel" into your conversations. All joking aside, shock dynamics is a great subject to learn, whether or not you intend to race your Pro Touring car on a regular basis.

Track Locator

A track locator is only necessary in a multi-link rear suspension system; it controls lateral movement of the rear-end housing. One end of the track locator attaches to a point

shocks are always advised on a Pro Touring build, but if you're going all out you'll likely use a pair of coil-over shocks on the rear, in combination with a multi-link setup.

It's important to know what the rear shocks are *not* responsible for, to get a better understanding of their purpose. They are not designed to control weight transfer or support the weight of the car. The real purpose of a shock absorber is to tame the spring movements to ensure a smooth suspension cycle. If the spring and shock combination is correct, you can adjust one or the other to affect the car's handling and grip.

Shock valving is an important aspect of the entire suspension package. The term *valving* refers to the movement of fluid in the shock absorber. Moving this fluid at different rates causes the shock to behave

differently in terms of how it compresses and how it rebounds. Valving affects the ride quality as well as the handling capabilities, so Detroit Speed

A track locator prevents lateral movement of the rear-end housing. In this case, a Panhard bar is used, providing a rigid backbone to keep the suspension free of any harmful side-to-side movement. The Panhard bar is adjustable to fine-tune the location of the rear end.

The Watt's linkage is a form of track locator that consists of two lateral bars connected to the rear end with a bell crank. This Z design acts as two independent track locators that keep the rear end stable throughout the full range of motion.

Anti-Roll Bar

An anti-roll bar is an essential piece of making a suspension work well. Many muscle cars came from the factory without a rear anti-roll bar, which means the car relies solely on the springs and shocks to keep the car level. Although a front anti-roll bar is far more important, a rear anti-roll bar is a welcome addition to any Pro Touring build. The rear anti-roll bar can be used to tune how the car "rotates" through the corners. The stiffer the rear anti-roll bar, the better the car rotates. The term most often used in this situation is making the car "freer" or "looser" in the corners. Likewise, if the car rotates too freely, a softer rear anti-roll bar rate can be used to "tighten" the handling.

Rear anti-roll bars reduce body roll without hindering ride quality or affecting everyday driving. An anti-roll bar on a car with leaf-spring suspension isn't going to work nearly as hard as an anti-roll bar on a car with multi-link rear suspension and coil springs. The leaf springs provide a bit more stability than coils but that's not to say that you can't put a sway bar on a car with leaf springs. Ultimately, a rear anti-roll bar helps any car reduce body roll through the corners.

It is important to know that the rear bar should be sized appropriately, so as not to create an oversteer condition, where the rear tires lose grip because of a lack of side-to-side weight transfer. An anti-roll bar that is too stiff creates oversteer by preventing sufficient weight transfer to plant the rear tires. The anti-roll bar must coincide with the overall weight of the car as well as the spring rates. Heavier cars tend to require a larger (stiffer) anti-roll bar to support the car's overall weight.

on the chassis, while the other end attaches to a bracket on the rear-end housing. The simplest form of track locator is known as a Panhard bar, which is a bar that travels with the suspension but resists any side-to-side movement of the rear end. You may have also heard this referred to as a track bar.

Another form of track locator is known as a Watt's linkage. It is truly old-school technology (we're talking 1780s) but it is a perfectly acceptable way to control lateral movement in the rear suspension. It consists of two horizontally oriented rods that connect to a center bell crank, which pivots on a given point on the rear-end housing. This Z configuration acts as two separate Panhard bars attached to a central location, which provides more effectiveness throughout the suspension cycle.

Regardless of your preference of a standard Panhard bar or a Watt's link-age, you have an important decision to make on the attachment points of the track locator. Most generic suspension kits feature a Panhard bar with nonadjustable attachment points with rubber bushings. If you're serious about being able to fine-tune the rear suspension, you won't like the idea of a fixed track locator.

Most Watt's linkages feature spherical rod ends (known as Heim joints), which thread into each end of the bars, offering adjustability. The drawback to rod ends is their short life span and the fact that they make a lot more noise than a regular rubber bushing.

Other systems, such as Detroit Speed's QUADRALink rear suspension, feature a Panhard bar with rubber bushings. The rubber bushings are more street friendly, and Detroit Speed's Panhard bar is adjustable because the ride height changes to control the car's roll center.

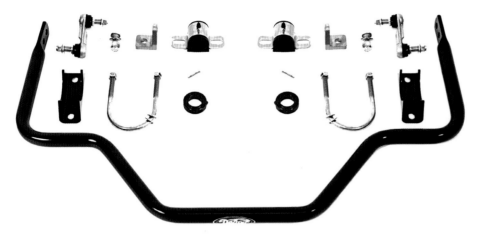

Many muscle cars and pony cars did not come from the factory with rear anti-roll bars. If you're planning to keep your build simple, a rear anti-roll bar install is a great place to start, but it's also an essential component for any hardcore Pro Touring build.

Installing an anti-roll bar is generally an easy task. It requires some drilling and minor fabrication work but the rear bar provides instant results without major effort or investment. Detroit Speed's anti-roll bars feature two mounting holes for the end links, offering two spring rates.

adjustable. The first-generation F-Body 1⅛-inch tubular bar features 344 pounds per inch when the end links are mounted in the front hole and 402 pounds per inch when mounted in the rear hole. The larger 1¼-inch bar features 496 pounds per inch in the front hole and 580 pounds per inch when mounted in the rear hole.

Detroit Speed's rear anti-roll bar offerings for first- and second-generation F-Body cars only fit QUADRALink rear suspension kits. Detroit Speed's anti-roll bar offerings for other platforms can generally be adapted to the original rear suspension.

One of the great features on the Detroit Speed rear anti-roll bar is adjustability. It has two mounting holes, which changes the leverage of the bar, thus changing the bar's spring rate. Anti-roll bar spring rate isn't often a topic of discussion for an average Pro Touring build but it's pretty important, and you can dial it in if the rear anti-roll bar is

Project: QUADRALink Rear Suspension Installation

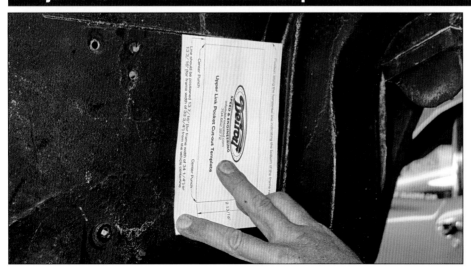

1 *Detroit Speed provides templates for all the necessary cuts to install the QUADRALink kit. Make the marks for the upper link pocket and get ready to let the sparks fly.*

2 Use templates to mark the necessary cuts on the top side of the floorpans. It helps to have a clean working area, so use an air grinder to sand these areas to the bare metal.

3 Use a cut-off wheel to remove the marked sections of metal. Be careful to leave a bit of wiggle room; it's better to come back and trim it to fit than to cut too much on the first try.

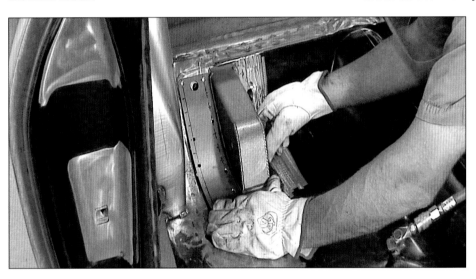

4 The upper link pocket, provided with the QUADRALink kit, can be placed over the cut-out area and inspected for fitment. This pocket will be plug-welded and then stitch-welded in several places, using a Miller MIG welder.

5 This is what the finished upper link pocket should look like after welding is complete. Seam sealer can be used around the edge of the spring pockets to keep debris from collecting between the floorpans and pockets.

6 Detroit Speed provides a Panhard bar bracket with the QUADRALink kit, which welds to the rear frame rail. The other end of the bar attaches to a bracket on the rear-end housing.

7 Part of the mini-tub process covered in Chapter 3 is installing a new raised crossmember that mounts between the wheel tubs. This allows clearance for the rear-end housing, and also provides a sufficient mounting point for the coil-overs.

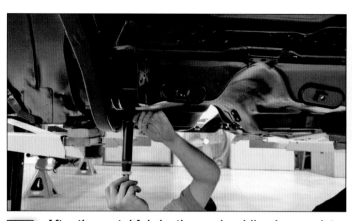

8 After the metal fabrication and welding is complete, it's a simple matter of bolting the parts together. The control arms are a tight fit in the pockets. Slide the arms into place and push the retaining bolt through to keep it from falling.

9 The lower control arms attach to a bracket that is included in the QUADRALink kit. Bolt the arms to the bracket before the bracket is installed on the car. Do not torque the bolts that fasten the control arm to the bracket just yet. These will be tightened to 120 ft-lbs of torque when the car is sitting at ride height.

10 The mounting bracket bolts to the outside of the frame rails and is held in place with three bolts. Note that the aluminum spacer for the control arm is located toward the rocker panel when the mounting bracket is in place.

11 With all four control arms hanging loosely in place, lift the rear-end housing and attach it to the arms. It's easiest to attach the lower arms first, and then rotate the housing to attach the upper arms. This is definitely a good time to grab a helping hand.

12 Attach the upper arms to the rear-end housing using the supplied hardware. Do not fully tighten the bolts at this point; they will be torqued to 120 ft-lbs when the car is at ride height.

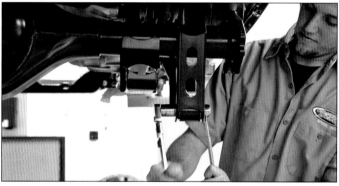

13 Use a 13/16-inch wrench and socket to tighten the bolts on both ends of all four arms. The front side of the upper links must be tightened from inside the car.

14 Air tools can be used to speed up this installation but it's much more precise to do the work by hand. It's easier to notice issues, such as binding, when installing nuts and bolts with simple hand tools. After the installation is complete and the car is at ride height, torque the control arm bolts to 120 ft-lbs.

15 The Panhard bar can now be installed. One side bolts to a bracket on the rear-end housing, and the other bolts to a bracket that is welded to the passenger-side frame rail. Installing the brackets takes much more time and effort than installing the bar itself. The bar can be adjusted later.

16 The coil-over brackets from the QUADRALink kit double as a mounting location for the anti-roll bar, making this an easy install because you can hold the bar in place and mark the holes for the mounting brackets. Attach the end links to the frame rail.

17 Next are the coil-over shocks, which bolt into place, thanks to Detroit Speed's supplied brackets. Final adjustments to the springs and shocks will be made at ride height.

18 It's always important to adjust the Panhard bar to center the rear-end housing. This ensures that the tire and wheel clearances are correct, and you obviously want the car to track straight as it goes down the road.

19 The kit comes with rear sway bar mounting brackets, which mount to the rear frame rail. The end link attaches to the large center bolt, and the two outer bolts hold the bracket in place.

Using Mac Martin's 1969 Camaro COPO as an example, this is the finished product, after the tires and wheels have been installed. You'll also notice the tight exhaust routing. It's the price you pay to have a great stance.

Another view of the finished QUADRALink setup provides a look at those massive 335/30ZR18 tires. A big footprint certainly increases traction, and it also gives the car the perfect Pro Touring stance and attitude.

BRAKES

Brakes get abused on a daily driver but it can be even worse with a Pro Touring car. If you're serious about a Pro Touring build, make sure the braking system is up to par on your car. The braking system on a Pro Touring build is just as important as the chassis and suspension modifications. If you're out on the autocross course or road course, a great suspension keeps the car stuck to the racing surface, but without a tough set of brakes, you're destined for trouble.

The fact of the matter is that most of our beloved Pro Touring platforms started life with drum brakes, sometimes on all four corners. Although a drum brake is safe for regular street driving, it does not provide the performance that a simple disc brake upgrade can provide. Even the cheap disc brake conversion kits provide a performance gain, but if you throw a few more dollars at the situation, you can have a high-end braking system that will withstand whatever you put it through.

For a Pro Touring build, disc brakes on all four corners are a must, and you'll likely want something a little more powerful (and durable) than original-style brakes, even if your car came from the factory with discs. Original disc brake systems from the 1960s and 1970s are not what most folks consider usable for Pro Touring purposes. The single-piston caliper is not ideal, the small-diameter rotor is not ideal, and the cast-iron master cylinder is not ideal. Throw that stuff into the swap meet pile and start from scratch with a purpose-built braking setup.

Pro Touring braking setups need to stop fast and stop often without fade or damage. A drum brake cannot withstand the abuse and a stock disc brake is not capable of surviving through major heat cycles and intense situations. You might think that the master cylinder is the least important part of the equation, but aftermarket master cylinders help the braking system function better. There is no question that a Pro Touring build requires a complete brake rebuild. This chapter includes step-by-step tips on reviving the muscle car's braking system from start to finish.

Tightly tucked inside an 18-inch wheel, the Baer 14-inch rotors and six-piston calipers provide immense braking power for this 1969 Camaro. Note the direction of the cross-drilled holes and slots. Baer rotors have the slots angled toward the front of the car, whereas those from other popular brake manufacturers are turned toward the rear.

Pro Touring cars must accelerate quickly and decelerate quickly, so most builds utilize a set of large-diameter disc brakes on all four corners. Autocross racing is tough on brakes; the courses are generally filled with straight stretches and sharp corners to provide a great challenge for muscle cars.

This is what you find beneath most muscle car and pony car applications. Drum brakes are never a good option for high-performance driving, especially in the Pro Touring world. Many cars came with disc brakes on the front and drums out back but it's always best to convert to four-wheel discs.

Rotors

Rotor size is important; a larger rotor provides more surface area for the brake pads. It's common to see 13- and 14-inch rotors on most Pro Touring builds but a large brake setup requires a 17-inch or larger wheel, so choose wisely. In most cases, a brake system that uses a 13-inch rotor requires the use of a 17-inch wheel, and as the brake rotor diameters go up, so do the minimum wheel diameter requirements. It's not the rotor that comes in contact with the wheel, it's the caliper; it's a general rule of thumb that the wheel diameter must be at least 4 inches larger than the brake rotor diameter. Many wheel manufacturers take great care to shape the spoke in a manner that helps with brake clearance because many Pro Touring braking systems use a large caliper.

Rotors have come a long way since the first disc brake was introduced. Because rotor strength, durability, and efficiency is always at the forefront of engineering and design, the rotors you can get today are more than sufficient for a 3,200-pound Camaro. High-performance brake rotors generally have some sort of heat evacuation system, and it's usually in the form of vents sandwiched between the two rotors, as well as slots and holes in the face of the rotor.

These measures allow the heat to escape the steel rotor so that the pads continue to grip the surface.

This rear-end setup features a Baer disc brake kit. The one-piece rotor slides over the wheel studs, and then a four-piston caliper and mounting brackets are bolted to the rear end. This is a great setup for any Pro Touring build; it's an easy install with a noticeable difference in stopping power.

If your muscle car came from the factory with disc brakes, this is probably what they look like. A heavy one-piece hub and brake rotor assembly measures 11 inches in diameter, offering sufficient braking for the 1960s era but nowhere near the capability of today's components.

As with many debates in the car world, there is an ongoing battle over brake rotors. Some folks say that slotted, undrilled rotors (left) are the way to go, but many others use a drilled and slotted rotor to evacuate as much heat as possible from the braking surface. Detroit Speed suggests drilled and slotted rotors for street applications, and undrilled rotors for more hardcore race-ready applications. Extreme heat cycles can cause the drilled rotors to crack.

Although an undrilled rotor has more surface area for the pad to contact, a cross-drilled rotor helps reduce heat in heavy braking situations. It also helps reduce weight, which is always a plus, but the limited surface area can cause cracking between the holes. This cracking is only common in hardcore builds that see extreme use.

Although most brake pads need heat to work efficiently, too much heat can cause the pads to deteriorate or glaze over, losing their friction.

Along with heat and gas evacuation, the slots and holes provide more bite for the brake pads, even though the total surface area is decreased. Slotted and cross-drilled rotors are suggested for all Pro Touring builds but beware of the cheap aftermarket rotors you might find at the auto parts store or on eBay. These rotors are thin and they do not perform at the level of a high-quality brake component from companies such as Baer or Wilwood.

Hardcore Detroit Speed builds receive slot-only rotors. This helps evacuate the used pad gases without the worries of cracking under extreme use, which can be a problem with drilled rotors. In other words, drilled rotors are ideal for street use but hardcore track time puts additional stress on the metal that can lead to cracking.

Some rotors feature a one-piece design, which generally slides over the hub and wheel studs. Others feature a two-piece design that uses a "hat" that mounts to the spindle; the rotor then bolt to the hat. On many standard GM applications, the front

Brakes get abused on Pro Touring cars, so pick your poison. Stacy Tucker's 1969 Camaro test car features 14-inch two-piece rotors with slots only. In this speed-stop challenge, Stacy clamps down on the front rotors and slides the front tires, obviously not the ideal method of stopping but brake bias can be changed with a proportioning valve.

hat houses the wheel bearings and doubles as a hub. Either design works well in a Pro Touring environment. It's mainly a matter of the application and how the particular brake rotor attaches to the car.

Common brake rotor problems are warping and cracking. Warping is caused by insufficient strength in the metal, combined with overheating and repetitive use. You can feel a warped rotor in the brake pedal, and if it's one of the front rotors, you can feel a lot of side-to-side movement in the steering wheel. Cracking is also a sign of overheating or hard abuse. This condition is common for cheap, aftermarket cross-drilled rotors; they are not generally constructed with high-quality steel.

Calipers

Offering clamping force on the brake pads, the calipers are another important component of the Pro Touring brake setup. Here's how they work: A burst of brake fluid is sent through the lines when the brake pedal is pressed, and this fluid moves a piston, which pushes the brake pad closer to the rotor. The pads apply pressure to the rotor with enough force to bring the car to a halt. The caliper is mounted in a fixed location: For the front, it mounts to the spindle upright, and for the rear, it mounts to the rear-end housing.

When disc brakes were first used on American automobiles, the calipers were clunky and inefficient, but they certainly outperformed drum brakes on all levels. As the years went by, caliper design evolved, providing better stopping power by increasing clamping force. What started as a single-piston design is now commonly available in four- and six-piston designs. Multiple pistons disperse the load evenly and provide a much larger clamping area than did the older designs.

Originally, brake calipers were made from cast iron. One of the biggest breakthroughs involved developing an aluminum caliper for

Brake calipers have evolved over the years, and it's common to see a Pro Touring car sport a set of six-piston aluminum calipers. What was once considered high end is now commonplace, but it's still a very important part of a Pro Touring build. These Baer 6R calipers are a work of art and provide unmatched stopping power.

Caliper clearance is often an issue when using aftermarket braking systems. Many muscle cars came from the factory with 14- or 15-inch wheels but a typical aftermarket disc brake setup requires at least a 17-inch wheel to clear the caliper. In this case, the six-piston caliper is a fairly tight fit, even on an 18 x 10–inch wheel.

Even though six-piston calipers are all the rage in the Pro Touring world, most cars do not need that much braking power on all four corners. Most builders combine the six-piston caliper up front with a four-piston caliper out back for the perfect combination.

high-performance applications. This reduces weight and offers a more efficient design to increase braking performance dramatically. Today's aftermarket brake caliper, a Baer 6S unit for example, features stainless steel pistons with staggered piston sizing to minimize brake pad wear. These details, in combination with the extreme surface area, result in an awesome braking system that looks cool too. It's hard to dislike the appearance of a big six-piston caliper tucked behind the spokes of a large-diameter wheel.

The heat dissipation, clamping force, and surface area are the main concerns of a disc brake caliper, so if you can order a brake kit that finely executes those details, expect to bolt it on and feel a big difference. A large rotor and a six-piston aluminum caliper go a long way to mak-ing your Pro Touring machine stop and handle like a modern sports car, but you must complete the brake system with matching components and accessories to make it all work in harmony.

Pads

A set of replacement brake pads might be sufficient for your daily driver or weekend cruiser but they just don't cut it in the Pro Touring world. Original-style brake pads are not aggressive enough to provide the appropriate clamping force, so many companies offer custom pads for various applications. A pad for short-course racing (autocross) may feature a different compound than that of a road race car that sees lots of heat cycles from heavy braking and multiple laps on the track.

Pad installation is the same as with a regular daily-driver brake job; the only trick is selecting the correct pads for your application. An aggressive "racing" brake pad is designed to work well under high-heat situations, so using them on the street is not advised. In addition to this, an aggressive brake pad needs to be teamed with a sticky tire to provide the best stopping power without locking the tires. Aggressive pads also have a very short life and can lead to premature wear on the rotors, while leaving the wheels covered in brake dust.

If you buy a brake kit, even from a trusted vendor such as Baer or Wilwood, it will likely come with a set of street brake pads. These pads are very friendly in regular driving conditions but don't expect them to do what you want in high-heat situations. Some companies, such as EBC Brakes, offer various brake pad compounds to help enthusiasts dial in the perfect amount of bite and streetability.

EBC is popular because of its clever pad compound designations. Greenstuff is the least aggressive, meaning that it's the hardest compound. That translates to long life but it doesn't quite have the bite of a softer, race-style brake pad. You can always step up to Redstuff, Bluestuff, Yellowstuff, and Orangestuff pads, depending on how serious you get with the setup.

Various materials are used in pad design, and some are more aggressive than others. The disadvantage of a soft-compound brake pad is a short life expectancy, as well as extreme amounts of brake dust. A good middle-of-the-road brake pad for street performance and moderate track day or autocross use is the EBC Yellowstuff pad.

Brake pads are often forgotten in the sea of shiny metal and fancy components that make up a Pro Touring car. Most aftermarket brake kits come with a set of street brake pads but many hardcore enthusiasts want a more aggressive pad with more bite.

An aggressive brake pad grips the rotor with the most force, but it also wears out quicker and coats the wheels in brake dust after a few hard stops. A medium-compound pad is suggested if you plan to drive your car on the street, and occasionally hit the autocross.

Master Cylinder

Another item that is easy to overlook is the master cylinder. An original cast-iron master cylinder does a great job for a stock braking system but it cannot keep up with the demands of a modern aftermarket disc brake setup. You need efficient fluid movement, and many aftermarket master cylinders can provide that with a very simple installation process. A couple of mounting bolts and the attachment of a couple of brake line fittings and you're good to go.

A modern-style master cylinder is always suggested on a Pro Touring build. Detroit Speed suggests using a 1-inch-bore master cylinder for the appropriate pedal feel and braking performance. Some aftermarket master cylinders feature an all-aluminum design, whereas others feature a late-model GM configuration with an aluminum cylinder body and plastic reservoir. There isn't a major advantage to either design, so your choice can be based on price or appearance. Luckily, master cylinders are one of the few components in a muscle car or pony car that interchange between any of the Big Three American auto manufacturers.

Manual versus Power

So you're ready to pull the trigger on an aftermarket master cylinder but you're unsure of using a brake booster. It's a common debate for muscle cars in general, but for the Pro Touring crowd the assistance of a power booster is more than welcome. It helps multiply the efforts of the brake pedal, meaning that you don't have to bear down as much to make it stop.

One of the biggest issues with manual brakes is a stiff pedal. To make a panic stop, or an aggressive stop on the autocross course, you'll feel as if the brake pedal is going to bend. Part of the reason for the stiff pedal in some manual brake applications is a mismatched master cylinder bore size. The larger the bore, the stiffer the pedal: If you use a master cylinder with a 1⅛-inch bore, the pedal will be stiff without power assistance.

Detroit Speed suggests a dual-diaphragm 9-inch brake booster because it's much more compact than some of the original General Motors, Ford, and Chrysler designs. It's also important to note that Detroit Speed's Brake Booster & Master Cylinder kit comes with an appropriately sized brake pedal pushrod and works with the original brake pedal. Most original and aftermarket pushrods are adjustable to properly locate the brake pedal and provide the correct amount of travel to take full advantage of the master cylinder.

A vehicle with very radical camshaft specs may suffer with a power brake setup: A shortage of engine vacuum may result in a shortage of vacuum inside the booster. This obviously isn't ideal but it generally isn't an issue with most modern engine combinations, even when an aftermarket camshaft is installed. Camshafts in modern engines do not need to be radical to make great horsepower, so most late-model engines have sufficient vacuum for power brakes.

Sending brake fluid to the calipers seems like a pretty straightforward task but the delivery system still needs attention on most muscle cars. Detroit Speed suggests a 1-inch-bore master cylinder to provide a firm pedal and plenty of fluid movement. This master cylinder is a late-model GM unit with a plastic reservoir.

Another braking debate argues the effectiveness of a manual master cylinder versus a power-assisted master cylinder. Although manual setups, such as this one, are mandatory on vehicles that do not have sufficient vacuum pressure to operate the booster, Detroit Speed suggests a 9-inch dual-diaphragm power booster.

A hydro-boost setup uses the power steering system to provide fluid to a cylinder inside the polished housing. This is a good option for engines with large camshafts, superchargers, or turbochargers because these engines lack the necessary vacuum for standard boosters. The disadvantage is loss of brake feel through the pedal.

If you run into an issue where the engine is robbing all of the vacuum, you can install a belt-driven vacuum pump, or possibly use an electric or hydraulic brake booster. Detroit Speed suggests retaining a vacuum-style booster.

Lines, Hoses and Fittings

When you're making a parts list for your Pro Touring brake rebuild, remember that lines, hoses, and fittings are important in tying the braking system together. New hard lines and flex hoses are a must for any brake build (even a stock rebuild) but they are especially important when you're dealing with a high-performance build. Pre-bent stainless steel hard lines are available

Chances are likely that a pre-bent brake line kit is available for your Pro Touring project. However, you'll never have results such as this sanitary setup with pre-bent tubing. Hand-bending your own tubing allows you to neatly arrange the lines, giving your car a more detailed appearance.

for most applications but you can easily make your own lines with a simple tubing bender and flare tool. Mild steel is much easier to bend and flare than stainless steel. In terms of performance, the mild steel and stainless steel are very close, but the stainless steel always costs you a few bucks more.

All disc brake setups feature a flexible hose that connects the hard brake line to the caliper, allowing the suspension and steering to cycle without disrupting the flow of brake fluid. Flex hoses should be constructed of braided stainless steel, rather than stock-style rubber hoses with steel ends. Most applications feature two flex hoses for the front (one for each caliper) and one flex hose for the rear, which connects the hard line to the rear distribution block attached to the rear-end housing.

Custom hoses and fittings can be made at race shops. Select parts

This rear end features a brass distribution block with one inlet from the braided stainless steel flex hose, and two outlets for the stainless steel hard lines. The hard lines extend to the ends of the rear-end housing, where they are mated to flex hoses and attached to the rear calipers using banjo fittings. Most cars originally equipped with drum brakes have hard lines that run all the way to the wheel cylinder. Rear disc brake conversions typically feature flexible lines.

stores with the capability to build hydraulic hoses for industrial equipment can build custom hoses as well. For the most part, braided hoses for use in braking applications can be sourced from any aftermarket brake parts supplier.

Proportioning Valve

Although brake lines, hoses, and fittings are very important in a Pro Touring application, there's another valuable piece to the puzzle: the proportioning valve. Originally, most muscle cars came with a brake distribution block, which determined how much fluid went to each line. It also served as a splitter, as most master cylinders have two outlets and a total of three hard lines (two front and one rear). These blocks are generally used on applications with disc brakes on the front and drums on the rear, in an effort to send the appropriate amount of fluid to each corner.

There is a lot to be gained with an aftermarket proportioning valve, which allows you to determine the brake bias on your vehicle with a twist of a knob. If you're serious about doing some autocross racing or road racing, you need to dial in the brake bias to keep one end from braking harder than the other. It's not ideal for the rear brakes to overpower the fronts in most situations, so the proportioning valve is installed inline with the rear brake lines to provide adjustability of the brake bias.

An adjustable proportioning valve can usually be fine-tuned and then left untouched, but many racers mount the proportioning valve within arm's reach to adjust the brake bias on the fly in compensation for changing track conditions, fuel burn-off, and tire wear.

Fluid

While we're on the subject of brake lines, let's talk brake fluid. It's what makes the brakes function, so yeah, it's pretty important. There are several types of fluid. These are the most popular: DOT 3, DOT 4, and DOT 5.

Most Pro Touring builds should use either DOT 3 or DOT 4. They perform the best with a wide range of components, from stock to highly modified. DOT 5 brake fluid has a high silicone content, which has

Here we go again with braking debates. This time it's regarding the type of fluid used in a braking system. DOT 3 is universal for most systems but it has a much lower boiling point than DOT 4, and therefore isn't suggested for high-performance builds. DOT 5 is not recommended because it can cause corrosion in the lines and calipers.

the advantage of a very high boiling point, but it has also been proven to cause corrosion in the lines and calipers if any moisture is introduced into the fluid.

The recommended fluid for the Pro Touring build is DOT 4 because it has a higher boiling point than DOT 3 but doesn't have the corrosive nature of DOT 5. In serious race cars, DOT 5 is advised because of the high boiling point, and the extreme maintenance routines between each race.

For most Pro Touring builds, the brake fluid is not changed and flushed often, so less-corrosive fluids are advised.

Bleeding The Brakes

After the brake system is complete, it's very important to bleed the system. It's also important to bleed the brakes any time you experience a different feel in the brake pedal. Bleeding the brakes is always a great first step in any sort of brake troubleshooting process. It's very easy but you need a helping hand (or foot).

If you're starting with a brand-new dry master cylinder and/or calipers, pour the fluid in slowly to avoid aerating the fluid. When the master cylinder is full, have your helper slowly press the brake pedal until he

or she starts to feel some resistance on the pedal. Check the fluid level and continue slowly pumping the brake pedal. The pedal should continually get higher until the calipers are filled with fluid.

You need a small box-end wrench to loosen and tighten the bleeder. You also need a small piece of clear hose to slide over the end of the bleeder. The hose allows you to catch the fluid and see any air pockets or bubbles as the fluid comes out. Bleed the calipers in order of farthest away from the master cylinder to nearest. The first caliper to be bled is always the right (passenger's side) rear.

Have your helper pump the pedal slowly and then hold the pedal down. Be careful here: The goal isn't to press extremely hard, just enough to keep pressure on the system. With the pedal at a constant pressure, loosen the bleeder momentarily and the pedal goes to the floor. Do not release the pedal until the bleeder has been tightened. You may do this multiple times per caliper to ensure all air bubbles are out of the system, but keep tabs on the fluid level; you never want the system to go dry.

Repeat these steps on all four calipers and you should have a great-working brake system.

Project: Brake System Assembly

1 *Detroit Speed offers a clutch master cylinder and brake master cylinder mounting brackets for F- and X-Body cars. This can either be bolted into place, or it can be welded into place (shown) for a slick transition.*

2 *The 9-inch dual-diaphragm brake booster and GM master cylinder can now be bolted to the firewall. The master cylinder is a cast-iron dual-outlet unit that features a 1-inch bore.*

3 *The lines can be bent using a hand bender to get the precise fit for your vehicle. The angle markings on the bender always come in handy, especially if you're trying to replicate the bends.*

4 *After the lines are bent and cut to length, the ends can be flared before installation. The flare provides a tight seal when the fitting is tightened. Speaking of fittings, don't forget to slide the fitting into place before flaring the tubing.*

5 *You can easily hide the proportioning valve or simply mount it directly underneath the master cylinder for easy line routing. This also provides easy access to the adjustment knob.*

6 *On the bottom side, this first-generation Camaro is bare bones. The front suspension is assembled and the braking system can be put together. Notice the Corvette-style forged spindle; it requires different caliper mounts than a standard Camaro spindle requires.*

7 *Install two M14-2.0x40–mm bolts from the back side and tighten to secure the aluminum caliper bracket to the spindle. Torque these bolts to 110 ft-lbs.*

8 *The Baer brake rotor slides over the wheel studs and is temporarily held in place with a couple of hand-tightened lug nuts. The rotor measures 14 inches in diameter and features a slotted and cross-drilled design, as well as a lightweight two-piece construction.*

9 *Detroit Speed is using a Baer 6P kit on this particular car. The kit is complete with brake pads; you install them before sliding the caliper into place.*

10 *The calipers are fitted to the rotor with the bleeder pointing up and the mounting holes line up. Slight resistance should be felt as the caliper and pads slide across the rotor. If the caliper doesn't slide into place easily, inspect the pads for proper installation.*

11 *Two Allen-head bolts thread into the mounting bracket and hold the caliper in place. Tighten these bolts to 85 ft-lbs of torque.*

12 *A close view of the installed caliper shows the brake pads seated nicely against the rotor. At this point, the rotor should still be able to turn but with slight resistance because of the new pads.*

13 *Out back, slide the axles into the 9-inch Ford rear-end housing in preparation for the brake build. The axles on this rear end are held in place at the end of the rear-end housing, instead of the C-clip–style retainers in GM rear ends.*

14 *Bolt the one-piece aluminum bracket to the axle flange using four Grade-8 bolts and nuts. This backing plate serves as the caliper mount. It also holds the internal parking brake assembly, which is essentially a drum brake inside the hat.*

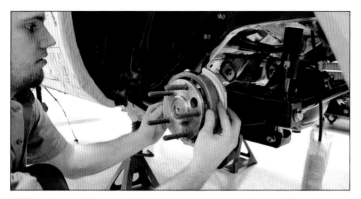

15 *Install the parking brake assembly by sliding the ends of the assembly over the parking brake actuator, which is already installed on the brake backing plate. The one-piece parking brake "shoe" is a tight fit around the axle flange and wheel studs.*

16 *With the parking brake shoe fitted properly, the two-piece 13-inch rotor can be installed. The rotor slides over the studs and is temporarily held in place with a couple of lug nuts.*

17 *Behind the rotor, bolt brake caliper mounts to the backing plate. Tighten the caliper bracket to 85 ft-lbs of torque using the supplied 12-mm bolts.*

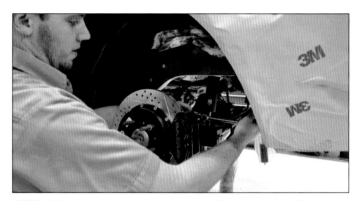

18 *The four-piston aluminum caliper can then be bolted to the mounting brackets using two Allen-head bolts. Keep in mind that the pads have not been installed.*

19 *With the caliper fitted, measure to find the offset of the caliper. Shims are provided with each brake kit, so measure the clearance on each side of the rotor to determine the shim width. If shims are not used to center the brake caliper on the rotor, the pads may not fit correctly.*

20 *Install the shims on the brake caliper bracket and then bolt it in place to center the caliper on the rotor. Now the brake pads can be installed, and the brake caliper can tightened to 75 ft-lbs of torque using the two supplied 12-mm bolts. This high-performance braking system is complete.*

CHAPTER 7

TIRES AND WHEELS

One of the most visible aspects of the Pro Touring movement is related to tires and wheels. Before Pro Touring, car guys were going to extreme measures to put large tires on their car, but it was only for the rear. Most ran narrow tires on the front and enormous tires out back to mimic the looks of a drag car. This was commonly known as the Pro Street look; it lasted quite a while and still has a bit of a following these days.

In the 1990s, many builders were stepping up to 17-inch wheel diameters, which was a big deal at the time. Only a few American auto manufacturers used 17-inch wheels, so when custom wheels hit the market, they sold like hot cakes. The problem was that most muscle car applications were limited to 7 or 8 inches in rim width. Some guys put large-diameter wheels on their car to be a part of the fad but others wanted more rubber

on the road. Mini-tubbing was necessary to get a wide tire under the rear, perpetuating a snowball effect of larger tires, larger tubs, wider wheels, etc.

By the mid-1990s, *Hot Rod* magazine had dipped its toe into the Pro Touring water, publishing stories about cars that were built to handle corners. Previously, articles in *Hot Rod* were limited to cars that performed well on the street or the drag strip. When the Pro Touring cars (sometimes called G Machines because of the G forces they could provide) hit the pages of major magazines, it was a huge wake-up call to the non-performers in the Pro Street world.

By 1993, Mark Stielow had built and abused his first Pro Touring build, helping start a movement that eventually turned into a legitimate market segment in the automotive aftermarket. Although the cars created a lot of buzz with their performance, the real wow factor was the stance and the tire and wheel combinations they used. A car that sits level and has wide tires on all four corners? Indeed.

Tire and wheel companies picked up on the new trend, and as

Large-diameter billet aluminum wheels and sticky high-performance tires are a Pro Touring car's most outstanding elements. This look has defined the market but still offers plenty of options for folks who are after a unique look. The most common Pro Touring wheel diameter is 18 inches but sizing is usually determined by brake diameter and the owner's taste.

It has always been cool to put a set of wide tires on a muscle car but they did it a little differently in the 1970s. Stock-width rear ends with 15 x 10–inch wheels and N50-15 tires were a popular look that often required extended shackles to provide ride height to clear the wide tires.

The evolution of wide tires eventually resulted in street cars with narrowed rear ends, huge rear tires, and superchargers protruding out of the hood. This trend was known as Pro Street, and it still has a cult following, even though it lost popularity in the 1990s, which is about the time Pro Touring came along.

Car guys love wide tires, and this is the typical Pro Touring footprint. This 1969 Camaro features a narrowed rear end, deep wheel tubs, QUADRALink rear suspension, and some extensive massaging to fit 20 x 12–inch wheels and 335/30R20 tires under the rear. The front tires are almost as wide, and the stance is very low, making for a very cool look.

with many things in the automotive world, they took it a bit too far. Incrementally going up in diameter, the wheels eventually passed up the performance threshold and moved into the "bigger must be better" category. Realistically, a Pro Touring car doesn't need anything larger than an 18-inch wheel. Most high-performance tires used on Pro Touring applications are available for 17- and 18-inch wheels but 18s are the norm.

Wheel diameter is pretty easy to figure out, but determining the rim width and all of the tire specifications can add some frustration to your selection process. Knowing how all of those numbers work with your car is the main thing. The following is a quick guide to tire and wheel sizing and how to make sure the rolling stock decision is a good one.

Tire Sizing and Ratings

For the most part, tires have a similar sizing system, with the only exception being full-on race tires. Most tires are designated using the P-metric system, meaning that the tire's width is displayed in millimeters, and the rim diameter is measured in inches. A P275/35R18 tire, for example, measures 275 millimeters in total width (or section width). The number "35" refers to the aspect ratio, which means the tire's sidewall height is 35 percent of its section width. The "18" refers to rim diameter.

P-metric sizing is the standard in modern tire building but it has changed greatly since the muscle car era. For instance, most muscle cars and pony cars featured tires with numeric and alphanumeric sizing, such as 7.35-14 or F70-14. To use alphanumeric as an example, the "F"

Tire sizing has changed over the years but the P-metric system is by far the standard system these days. A common size for the rear of a Pro Touring build is 335/30R18; it is generally the largest tire to fit with Detroit Speed's line of products.

The tire of choice for most hardcore Pro Touring enthusiasts is the BFGoodrich g-Force Rival. It's available in many relevant sizes, fitting wheels from 15 to 20 inches in diameter. The Rival tire is W-rated and features a Treadwear rating of 200, which is the softest tire allowed by some racing organizations.

actually designated the tire's load rating, which coincided with its overall size (the higher the letter, the larger the tire). The number "70" determined the aspect ratio (percentage) and the "14" is the wheel diameter, measured in inches.

To accurately choose the correct tires for your Pro Touring build, all of these numbers become very important, especially when you add a lowered ride height and the wheel dimensions into your equation. It can be quite frustrating but the goal is to fit the widest tire and wheel under the car without contacting the body or suspension components.

You'll notice a lot of stuff on the sidewalls of the tires, and it's all pretty important information. The size is obviously posted clearly on the sidewall but you'll also find information such as the UTQG rating, the load rating, max pressure, DOT numbers, warnings, and more.

You also want to consider the tire's ratings before pulling the trigger on a new set of shoes. Uniform Tire Quality Grade (UTQG) ratings are one of the first things to look at because these determine the treadwear grade, traction grade, and temperature grade. You might think that traction grade is the most important factor in the UTQG rating but it actually refers to the tire's *wet* traction, so that doesn't really apply. You can usually glean some *dry* traction information by the tire's treadwear grade, which tells a lot about the tire's traction compound.

A low treadwear number, such as 100, usually tells you the tire has a soft compound; a tire with a high number, such as 500, hints that the tire features a hard compound. The treadwear grade is determined by a standard testing procedure, which involves a 400-mile loop that results

much better than a medium or hard compound, it results in very quick tread wear, even in regular street-driving conditions.

in a total of 7,200 miles. If the tread lasts for only 7,200 miles, the treadwear is graded at 100; a grade of 200 indicates the tread should last twice as long. The previously mentioned example of a 500 treadwear grade would last five times as long, meaning its approximate tread life is 36,000 miles.

With these grades in mind, look for tires with a lower number because they feature a much softer compound to provide more traction. Some sanctioning bodies require a tire with a treadwear grade limit of 200, to keep super-soft race tires out of the running. BFGoodrich is the leader of the

Tires that have a treadwear rating lower than 200 generally have a soft compound. Although soft compounds grip the racing surface

If you're serious about racing, a little rubber splattered on the quarter panel shouldn't scare you. Usually it takes a lot of tire spin to result in this much rubber spray, but a hard day on the autocross course will certainly shave a few millimeters off the tread.

Burnouts are great fun, but when the tires cost more than $300 each, you'll likely keep the tire smoke to a minimum. It is common to see a Pro Touring car do a very small burnout to clean the rear tires before a run but tire smoke during the run is usually a bad thing.

market for Pro Touring tires, and has many purpose-built tires to meet the needs of racers and enthusiasts.

All modern tires feature a speed rating, which is the tire's tested maximum speed. Tire manufacturers perform tests that incrementally increase the speed (combined with the appropriate load) to determine the speed rating. This rating is designated by a single letter, such as "Z," which refers to a tire that is capable of 149 mph.

When Z-rated tires came onto the market, 149 mph seemed like a lot, and it is often regarded as the highest speed rating available. It is not. Although most Z-rated tires are advertised as such, many of them are actually W- or Y-rated, and capable of 168 and 186 mph, respectively. Tires with W- or Y-ratings often have the letter "Z" in the tire's size description: for example, P275/35ZR18.

Yes, it's somewhat confusing, but you could say the tire companies jumped the gun on the Z designation, assuming that 149 mph would be the max speed for a street tire, and had to backpedal to the W and Y ratings.

Wheel Sizing and Construction

Wheel sizing is a bit more straightforward than tire sizing, as it's measured in inches, and features three critical measurements: diameter, width, and backspacing. All three measurements are important but there aren't any major ratings or metric-to-standard measurement conversions to consider. One thing you want to remember is the size of the braking system, because many large aftermarket brake setups require a 17- or 18-inch wheel. Always consult the brake company and wheel company to make sure the components work together before ordering thousands of dollars' worth of parts.

Wheel diameter is measured on the bead seat (not the outermost flange). Width is also measured by the bead seat (not the overall width of the wheel). Backspacing is the measurement from the mounting surface (hub) of the wheel to the inside of the rim. An 18 x 8–inch wheel with 4 inches of backspacing, for example, has an equal amount of "dish" on the inner and outer por-

tion of the wheel. Many applications require custom backspacing dimensions to take advantage of every inch of space in the wheelhouse.

You may also hear the term *offset* used in regard to the spacing of wheels. Offset is the distance between the wheel mounting flange and the center of the wheel. This is usually measured in + or -, depending on the location of the mounting flange. Although many modern wheel manufacturers designate offset in wheel specifications, you can usually figure out the offset by measuring the backspacing.

If the wheel measures 18 x 10 inches and has 5 inches of backspacing, that equals zero (neutral) offset. Negative offset equals less backspacing (deep-dish look) and positive offset equals more backspacing (flat-faced look).

It isn't uncommon to see backspacing measurements as high as 8 inches in some applications but it's best to keep the center section of the wheel somewhere close to centered in the rim. For its first-generation Camaro builds, Detroit Speed generally runs an 18 x 10–inch wheel up

Wheel sizing varies greatly throughout the Pro Touring world but it seems as if it always comes back to 18-inch diameter as the most popular size. Widths still vary, depending on the amount of real estate available, but you can count on 8 inches being the bare minimum.

Although a few companies offer large-diameter steel wheels, aluminum is the material of choice for hardcore Pro Touring machines. If you like the looks of stock GM wheels, such as the popular Honeycomb wheel (middle), you can get large-diameter versions of these wheels in cast aluminum.

front with 6.125 inches of backspacing, and an 18 x 12–inch wheel on the rear with 5.50 inches of backspacing. This provides the deep-dish look that we all love, and puts plenty of rubber on the road. Backspacing measurements are different for every car, and the width of the rear-end housing plays a huge role in the wheel measurements.

In terms of wheel construction, you always want to go with a high-grade aluminum wheel for its strength and light weight. Some wheel manufacturers have created

large-diameter steel wheels, such as the Chevy Rallye, to give you the Pro Touring look with a classic design. These wheels look cool and they're built with very good quality in mind, but they are very heavy compared to the race-inspired aluminum wheels on the market. Weight reduction is a big part of going fast, and you shed a lot of unsprung weight and rotating mass by opting for a light tire and wheel combination.

Many years ago, wheel manufacturers used magnesium to build lightweight racing wheels. Although they were superbly light, they didn't have the durability and strength of an aluminum wheel. Most companies therefore converted their wheel manufacturing to aluminum. For instance, the first rendition of the wildly popular American Racing Torq Thrust wheel was constructed from magnesium but was later switched to cast aluminum in the 1960s.

Speaking of the term *cast*, you should also take note of the manufacturing style. In most cases, a cast-aluminum wheel is weaker and

Wheel sizing is usually limited by the amount of room in the wheelhouses. Most stock wheelhouses can only hold an 8-inch-wide wheel but the installation of mini-tubs can potentially allow a 12-inch-wide wheel. Sometimes, modifications to the rear frame rails are necessary to gain enough clearance.

This super-slick 1969 Mustang offers a great Pro Touring look, thanks to a slammed stance and 17-inch cast-aluminum wheels, which are made to replicate Shelby Cobra wheels from the 1960s. Upsized replica wheels are popular; they help retain the car's vintage flair while also providing the Pro Touring appeal.

As you can imagine, a large-diameter wheel can be quite heavy if it isn't constructed with the appropriate materials. Steel is certainly the heaviest option, adding to the car's rotating mass. Cast aluminum is second in line, offering great weight savings, but forged aluminum wheels are the lightest, strongest, and safest wheels on the market.

heavier than a forged aluminum wheel. On the other hand, cast wheels are generally less expensive, so they end up on lots of Pro Touring–style cars. Manufacturers such as Formula 43 and HRE provide top-notch forged aluminum wheels that can be custom tailored to fit your application.

What Will Fit?

So, you want the Pro Touring look but you're not sure if you can fit a set of wide tires and wheels in the con-

fines of your project car. It's a common problem. As gearheads, we always want to use every square inch of real estate for our tire and wheel package. If you're happy with using a set of off-the-shelf 18 x 8–inch wheels, you can probably get away with it. However, if you want the killer looks and performance of a wide combination, such as a 335/30R18 wrapped around an 18 x 12–inch wheel, mini-tubbing is the only option. It's good to know your limits and there's only one way to know for sure.

Regardless of your application, you need to take some time to mea-

sure for the appropriate tire and wheel size. It's very important to get these measurements before deciding on tires and wheels to determine the necessary backspacing. You can use a straightedge and a measuring tape to measure for the correct width and backspacing if you have a helping hand in the shop.

The straightedge always needs to be used to simulate the mounting surface of the wheel; you want it to rest against the front hub or the rear axle flange. Then, the measuring tape can be used to give you an idea of how much room you have on the front side of the straightedge and on the backside. This helps determine the maximum tire and wheel size. Always allow an inch on each side of the measurement for the tire's sidewall bulge; this also gives you some wiggle room in hard corners when the suspension flexes and articulates. Front tire and wheel clearance is crucial. Always perform the measurements with the steering wheel

You can easily measure for tire and wheel clearance at home with a straightedge and tape measure. Always measure tire and wheel clearance with the car at ride height. Start by measuring the distance from the wheel mounting point to the lip around the wheel opening.

Using the straightedge as a reference point to the wheel-mounting surface, measure inward to the wheel tub and frame rail. Repeat this measurement in several locations to ensure the proper backspacing on the wheels.

Up front, continue to use the straightedge and tape measure to determine the largest possible tire and wheel combination without interfering with the fenders, frame rails, or suspension components. Turn the steering wheel lock-to-lock and check clearances with the front suspension at ride height.

Because Pro Touring cars are constantly being thrown into corners and undergoing hard braking, it's important to account for these conditions when measuring for tire and wheel clearance. You can compress the suspension to replicate the approximate load and measure again to double-check clearances.

If you have a tire that matches your desired size, you can use a tool known as the Tire Mount Mate. It is adjustable, so you can see exactly what width and backspacing is needed to fit your car perfectly. It bolts to the hub and provides a nice visual that the straightedge and measuring tape cannot provide.

The range of adjustment on the Tire Mount Mate is great, and allows you to dial-in the perfect sizing. It's clearly marked and easy to use, but still remember to take notes so that you can spout off the measurements when you order the wheels.

straight, measure with the wheel turned all the way left and all the way right to determine any areas that might scrub under full steering lock.

If you don't want to fool with the old-school method of a straightedge and tape measure, you can order a Tire Mount Mate, which is an aluminum fixture that bolts to the hub. This tool allows you to measure for tire and wheel clearance by using an actual tire for reference. It is fully adjustable for various wheel diameters, widths, and backspacing measurements.

The Tire Mount Mate certainly helps when it comes to figuring out the backspacing measurements for your application, but other tools are also available. One example is the Percy's Wheelrite, which serves the same purpose as the Tire Mount Mate but features a cheaper plastic construction and a much lower price tag. The Tire Mount Mate comes in just under $400, whereas the Percy's Wheelrite is available at most vendors for less than $100.

What If They Don't Fit?

Sometimes car guys make mistakes. Part of our mindset is to figure out how to make the best of the situation. Just because a tire and wheel combination doesn't quite fit the car doesn't mean you've failed. This sort of thing has led to a number of cool

modifications. Who could forget the fender flares of the 1970s? They were the result of a tire and wheel that was a bit too wide for the body. Maybe that isn't the greatest example, but the following options may ease your mind.

First of all, some cars, such as any of the 1962–1967 Chevy II bodies, feature very small wheel openings. The length of the wheel opening looks strange when a large tire and wheel combination is used, so many people stretch the opening to accommodate the dimensions of the tire. This requires a moderate amount of fabrication and metalwork but it makes a huge difference in the appearance of the car if you're trying to stuff a huge tire and wheel in a tight spot. Sometimes, cars from the 1950s and early 1960s have the same sort of wheel opening issues in the rear, and for this reason I suggest mocking up the tire and wheel combination before completing the bodywork process.

Once you have the tires and wheels fitting properly in the wheel

Wheel & Tire Fitment	Front (Stock)		Front (DSE Subframe)		Rear (Stock)		Rear (DSE Mini-Tubs)	
	Wheel Size	Tire Size	Wheel Size	Tire Size	Wheel Size	Tire Size	Wheel Size	Tire Size
1967-1968 F-Body	17" x 8"	245/40ZR17	17" x 8"	245/40ZR17	17" x 9"	275/40ZR17	17" x 11"	315/35ZR18
	18" x 8"	245/40ZR18	18" x 9"	255/35ZR18	18" x 9"	275/40ZR18	18" x 11"	315/30ZR18
1969 F-Body	17" x 8"	245/40ZR17	17" x 8"	245/40ZR17	17" x 9.5"	275/40ZR17	17" x 12"	335/35ZR17
	18" x 8"	245/40ZR18	18" x 10"	275/35ZR18	18" x 9.5"	275/40ZR18	18" x 12"	335/30ZR18

This is the tire and wheel fitment chart that Detroit Speed uses to compare stock F-Bodies to F-Bodies that have a Detroit Speed subframe and mini-tubs.

opening, your next area of concern is the width and spacing of the wheel. An inch of backspacing can make a very big difference in the way a wheel fits, so it's always important to measure precisely. If you ordered the wheels with 1/2 inch too much backspacing, you can always use a wheel spacer to shim the wheel toward the outside of the car.

Wheel spacers are okay for use on a Pro Touring car, but always use a hub-centric spacer that bolts into place instead of the simple piece of steel that slides over the wheel studs. The washer-style spacers put too much load on the wheel studs. I've seen folks use spacers up to 4 inches wide but I don't recommend it. I'm most comfortable with wheel spacers that are 1 inch or less in width because these do not create safety concerns in most street applications. A car that has full-on road race tires and big-time horsepower may not be a great home for wheel spacers: the

more grip and power you apply, the more stress it puts on the spacer.

Now, let's reverse it and say the wheels *need* another 1/2 inch of backspacing, and the combination comes in contact with the lip around the wheel opening. There's also a way to help this problem, and it's something nearly every car guy has done at some point in his or her life. It's generally referred to as "rolling the lip." This is when you take the flange that folds under the wheel opening (usually at a 90-degree angle) and "roll" it out of the way. Some applications only need the lip rolled to about 120 degrees but I've seen many cars that had the lip folded completely over to 180 degrees. I would not suggest doing the full 180-degree fold unless you're completely out of options.

Rolling the lip can mean using a hammer and dolly to fold the flange (pre-bodywork and paint) or it can mean carefully folding the lip with a special tool if your car is already painted. Either way, the rear is much more difficult to roll, as it consists of two layers of steel, whereas the front fender is generally just a single stamping. Eastwood makes a fender-rolling tool that bolts to the hub and makes easy work of the rolling process. You

You can usually get away with a small sizing or spacing miscalculation by using a spacer or rolling the lips around the wheel opening for added clearance. Mac Martin's Camaro was so precisely done that he was able to retain the stock stainless steel wheel opening trim.

can also use a wooden baseball bat to roll the lip. The tire and wheel must be installed, and you roll the bat around the wheel opening, gradually applying more pressure with each pass. If you're rolling the lip on a car with finished paintwork, be sure to use a heat gun to warm the paint, to prevent cracks from the pressure.

Here's something that slips through the cracks during the tire and wheel measurement process: the side profile. Many cars, especially Tri-Five Chevys, early Chevelles, and Chevy IIs, suffer from short wheel openings. Stuffing an 18-inch wheel into this space can be tough, even with the short sidewalls of most high-performance tires.

Always measure from the front to the rear of the wheel opening if you have a radical tire and wheel combination. If you have a tire lying around the shop that closely resembles the diameter of your desired combination, mock it up to eyeball the look. This Chevy II has stretched wheel openings to accommodate massive tires and wheels.

If the outer wheel spacing is not severe enough to require rolling the lip, you can always trim the excess metal off the flange to gain 1/4 inch or more in some cases. On the rear, the quarter panel and inner structure are held together with a number of spot-welds; be sure to retain the welds and only trim off the excess metal on the flange.

A close look at this 1967 Camaro show car reveals severely trimmed lips around the wheel opening. Although it gave them another 1/2 inch of clearance, the modification nearly removed the lip entirely. Cutting too far into the lip can remove the welds that hold the quarter panel to the wheelhouse, which can cause all sorts of problems.

Vintage Corvettes are notorious for limited tire and wheel space. The original frame and suspension design is the limiting factor, so many enthusiasts go outward with the tire and wheel combination instead of inward. This car has very subtle body modifications to widen the quarter panels, and still only has enough room for 285/35R18 tires.

This particular front fender has approximately 1/4 inch trimmed from the lip, and you can see that the lip has also been folded over to gain even more clearance. Detroit Speed suggests rolling the fender and quarter panel lips during the metal fabrication process.

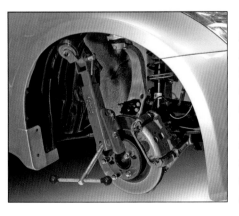

If you're dealing with a tire clearance issue on a car that is already body-worked and painted, you'll be forced to use a roller tool, such as this one from Eastwood. It bolts to the hub and uses a Delrin roller to gradually roll the lip. Eastwood suggests only using the roller on single panel areas, such as the front fender. (Photo courtesy of Eastwood)

When using a roller tool, always preheat the area to prevent the paint and underlying primers and fillers from cracking. Most of the time this method works well but be prepared to see some cracks if your car has any serious damage or rust that is covered up with body filler in the area. (Photo courtesy of Eastwood)

ENGINE AND DRIVETRAIN

Horsepower is something that every car guy wants, regardless of his favorite make, model, or style of car. Years ago, the recipe for big-time horsepower was high compression, high-lift mechanical camshafts, and huge carburetors, but today's high-tech engines can make the same amount of power and still manage to get more than 20 mpg. That's a significant reason that most Pro Touring cars feature a late-model engine. They're reliable, they're fast, and they're affordable.

Engine swaps are very common in the Pro Touring world; there is no shortage of aftermarket product support for items such as headers, oil pans, and motor mounts built specifically for modern engine swaps. There was a time when all of these components had to be fabricated to pull off a modern engine swap, and many instances still require heavy fabrication. It's all part of the process of updating the classic muscle car to today's standards, and you won't believe how much power these super-efficient fuel-injected engines are creating. This chapter provides some of those speed secrets, in addition to tips and tricks for installing a new engine into an old car.

All the talk about swapping a modern engine into an old car may be popular but it isn't mandatory to creating an acceptable Pro Touring car. An old-school small-block or big-block always fits into the high-performance world. Using what some might consider an outdated combination is nothing to be embarrassed about. If you're not ready to give up your older engine, you have many options, such as retrofit fuel injection systems, to update it and help it perform well on the street and at the track. Don't let the wiring intimidate you. Companies such as Holley, Edelbrock, and FAST are manufacturing bolt-on kits with self-tuning software that does all the hard work for you.

The biggest disadvantage old-school engine combinations face is weight. Modern engines generally have an aluminum block and

An updated small-block still catches a lot of attention and provides plenty of power. In this case, it features Inglese eight-stack fuel injection, which combines the vintage look with the convenience of electronic fuel injection. Take note of the super-clean engine bay. This car is very nicely detailed.

Engine swaps are a big part of the Pro Touring scene, and the king of engine swaps is Mark Stielow. He's a GM engineer, and he's built a number of outstanding Pro Touring beasts, all of which had modern engines. This one, Red Devil, features an LS7 with LS9 cylinder heads and supercharger setup.

It takes a lot of nerve to pull a perfectly good engine out of a classic muscle car but it's quite common when building a Pro Touring car. This second-generation Camaro had a good-running aluminum-headed small-block but it was yanked out in favor of a modern LS-based power plant.

This is the silver 1969 Camaro that we've followed throughout the book, and it had a "chalk-mark restoration." With a 427-ci big-block, it was a rare beast, but a cast-iron big-block isn't the ideal Pro Touring engine.

The most common form of engine swap involves the GM LS engine platform. These engines hit the streets in 1997 and the engine platform is still available in some GM vehicles. They are readily available and make tons of power, so an LS engine swap is a no-brainer for a Pro Touring build.

cylinder heads, and some form of composite or aluminum intake manifold. This sheds a significant amount of weight from the nose of the car to help with overall weight distribution. Of course, you can always upgrade to an aluminum block or cylinder heads on an old-school small-block or big-block, but at that point you're reaching deep into your pocketbook. Modern, fuel-injected engines certainly play a part in making an old car handle and perform as well as or better than a new Corvette. For this reason, late-model engine swaps are quite common.

GM LS-Series Engine

This book concentrates heavily on GM platforms, as they are the most common for Pro Touring builds. The choices are very broad for a new GM power plant. Take a look at all of the offerings in the LS family of engines and figure out which one is right for your ride. GM Performance Parts offers a number of LS-based crate engines, but you can also get modified LS engines from vendors such as Mast Motorsports.

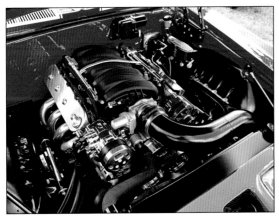

This is what a sanitary LS engine swap into a first-generation Camaro looks like. It has ceramic-coated headers, an aftermarket accessory system, and a custom radiator. None of these items are 100-percent necessary to perform the swap, but they certainly make for a much cleaner install. Relocating the coil packs is also a nice touch.

You can pick up a 5.3-liter Vortec engine for $500 to $1,000 (depending on mileage) from pretty much any junkyard to provide an awesome starting point for your project car. A regular LS1 intake bolts directly in place of the bulky truck intake, and you can also swap the accessory systems for a better fit. (Photo courtesy of General Motors)

If you're building on a tight budget, you can always pluck a Vortec truck engine out of a GM truck and build it yourself. Some guys are making serious power with truck engines, but be aware that they feature a cast-iron block that definitely creates a trade-off of weight versus cost. The most popular Pro Touring–friendly engines are the LS2, LS3, and LS7 because of their all-aluminum construction and big-time horsepower right out of the box.

Vortec Engines

Multiple versions of the Vortec-powered GM trucks and SUVs have displacements of 4.8, 5.3, 6.0, and 6.2 liters. The majority of Vortec engines utilize a cast-iron block and aluminum cylinder heads, and the camshaft grinds are geared more toward towing and efficiency than all-out performance. Most of the engines with the "LS" designation feature

GM LS Applications

LS4
5.3-liter, aluminum block, aluminum heads, 303 hp
2006–2009 Chevy Impala SS
2006 & 2007 Chevy Monte Carlo SS
2005–2008 Pontiac Grand Prix GXP
2008 Buick LaCrosse Super

LS1
5.7-liter, aluminum block, aluminum heads, 305 to 350 hp
1997–2004 Corvette (non Z06)
1998–2002 Chevy Camaro Z28 or SS
1998–2002 Pontiac Trans Am or Firebird Formula
2004 Pontiac GTO
Various Holden models in Australia

LS6
5.7-liter, aluminum block, aluminum heads, 385 hp (2001), 405 hp (2002–2005)
2001–2004 Corvette Z06
2004 & 2005 Cadillac CTS-V

LS2
6.0-liter, aluminum block, aluminum heads, 390 to 400 hp
2005 & 2006 Pontiac GTO
2005–2007 Corvette (non Z06)
2006–2009 Chevy Trailblazer SS
2006 & 2007 Cadillac CTS-V

LS3
6.2-liter, aluminum block, aluminum heads, 424 to 436 hp
2008–2013 Corvette (non Z06)

2009 Pontiac GT GXP
2010–present Chevy Camaro
2014 Chevy SS
Various Holden models in Australia

LSA
6.2-liter, aluminum block, aluminum heads, supercharged, 556 hp
2009–2013 Cadillac CTS-V
2012 Chevy Camaro ZL1

LS9
6.2-liter, aluminum block, aluminum heads, supercharged, 638 hp
2009–2013 Corvette ZR1

LS7
7.0-liter, aluminum block, aluminum heads, 505 hp
2006–2013 Corvette Z06

all-aluminum construction. From 1999 to 2014, GM used these engines in everything from full-size pickup trucks to large conversion vans.

Power output ranges from 285 to 403, depending on the model but your best bet for performance is the late-model 6.2-liter engines (L92) used in 2009 and newer GM SUVs. The L92 is all-aluminum and features variable valve timing. It makes 403 hp!

For most Vortec engine platforms, a simple camshaft and valve-spring swap, along with an LS6 intake manifold swap, makes great power without breaking the bank.

The New LT1

With all of the buzz words such as direct injection and variable valve timing entering the new car market, it is likely that some of these new engine offerings will make their way into the Pro Touring world. It's hard to imagine the LS engines being phased out of popularity by the "new LT1" (thanks GM, for making the LT1 moniker so confusing) that hit the streets in the 2014 Corvette, but the new technology is very impressive. The new LT1 certainly proves its potential with more than 450 hp on tap and fuel mileage near the 30-mpg mark. It's an incredibly well-engineered piece, and it will likely find its way into a Pro Touring car by the time this book hits the shelves.

Will the LT1 be a realistic engine option for your Pro Touring build? Maybe, but you have to wait for after-market support to help with pesky engine swap details, such as wiring, oil pan, headers, etc., because all of those features have changed from the LS family of engines. When the aftermarket support sees a demand, it creates an entirely new market, but

The Gen 5 LT1 made its debut in the 2014 Corvette and has already received a ton of aftermarket product support. This 6.2-liter engine features an all-aluminum construction, direct fuel injection, and variable valve timing. This platform may get a lot of attention but it will take many years of production to catch up with the LS family. (Photo courtesy of General Motors)

Ford Motor Company hit a home run when it slapped a Roots-style supercharge on top of its "mod motor." These supercharged overhead-camshaft engines came from the factory in production vehicles, such as the Lightning, GT, and Mustang Cobra. It doesn't take much to wake up these low-displacement, highly efficient engines.

don't expect the LS family of engines to disappear; they are way too reliable and affordable to be completely wiped off the radar.

Ford Modular Engine

The Ford guys also have plenty of choices, thanks to the modular engine design created by Ford in the early 1990s. The "mod motor" has a pretty big advantage over GM and Mopar offerings: It features an over-head cam design, which is highly efficient and allows for high-RPM durability.

Many Ford fans love the supercharged 4.6-liter DOHC engine that came in 2003 and 2004 SVT Cobras. They pack a lot of power and have lots of room to grow. The new king is the Coyote, a 5.0-liter mod motor that cranks out more than 400 hp without the use of a power adder.

Mod motors are readily available from junkyards if you want to go the

Swapping a mod motor into a classic Ford can be a bit of a headache because of the size of the engine and the width of the shock towers on most applications. Detroit Speed solved this problem with a custom front suspension setup that gets rid of those pesky shock towers.

budget route, or you can call up Ford Racing for a wide selection of crate engines, including the new Coyote 5.0-liter engine.

Modern Hemi Engine

Mopar lovers are a distinct group, and they also have plenty of options for a modern engine swap. Their engine choice is quite possibly the most popular four-letter word in the go-fast industry: *Hemi*. The new Hemi hit the scene in 2003, and it's been placed under the hood of millions of cars, trucks, and SUVs under the Chrysler umbrella of brands. You can get a great deal on a junkyard Hemi, and expect it to crank out nearly 400 hp. These engines run well and they look cool, so they're a perfect fit for a Mopar Pro Touring ride. Mopar

Ford Mod Motor Applications

4.6-liter SOHC Two Valve
Iron block, aluminum heads,
190 to 260 hp
1991–2011 Lincoln Town Car
1992–2012 Ford Crown Victoria
1994–1997 Ford Thunderbird
1994–1997 Mercury Cougar
1997–2010 F-series pickup
1997–present E-series van
1996–2004 Mustang (non-Cobra)
2002–2005 Ford Explorer

4.6-liter SOHC Three Valve
Iron or aluminum block, aluminum heads,
292 to 315 hp
2005–2010 Ford Mustang (aluminum
block)
2006–2010 Explorer (cast-iron block)
2007–2010 Explorer Sport Trac
(cast-iron block)
2009–2010 Ford F-series pickup
(cast-iron block)

4.6-liter DOHC Four Valve
Iron or aluminum block, aluminum heads,

260 to 390 hp
1993–1998 Lincoln Mark VIII
1995–2002 Lincoln Continental
1996–2001 Mustang SVT Cobra
2003 & 2004 Mustang SVT Cobra
(cast-iron block, supercharged)
2003 & 2004 Mustang Mach 1
2003 & 2004 Mercury Marauder
2003–2005 Lincoln Aviator

5.0-liter "Coyote" DOHC Four Valve
Aluminum block, aluminum heads, 412
to 420 hp
2011–present Mustang GT

5.0-liter Boss 302 Four Valve
Aluminum block, aluminum heads, 444 hp
2012–present Boss 302 Mustang

5.4-liter SOHC Two Valve
Iron block, aluminum heads, 255 to 380
hp
1997–2004 Ford F-series pickup
1997–2004 Ford Expedition

1997–present Ford E-series van
1999–2004 Ford SVT Lightning
(supercharged)

5.4-liter SOHC Three Valve
Iron block, aluminum heads,
300 to 320 hp
2004–2010 Ford F-series pickup
2005–present Ford Expedition
2005–present Lincoln Navigator

5.4-liter DOHC Four Valve
Iron or aluminum block, aluminum heads,
300 to 550 hp
1999–2004 Lincoln Navigator
2000 Mustang SVT Cobra
2005 & 2006 Ford GT (supercharged)
2007–2012 Mustang GT500 (supercharged)

5.8-liter DOHC Four Valve
Aluminum block, aluminum heads,
supercharged, 662 hp
2013–present Mustang GT500

of 50-percent gains in horsepower with accompanying fuel system and ECM upgrades. This modern Hemi puts down more than 500 hp to the rear tires.

As with any of the engines listed in "Modern Hemi Applications" (below), the new Hemi responds very well to boost. Roots or twin-screw superchargers can often provide upward

Performance offers a number of options for crate engines and accessories for the new Hemi, so crunch the numbers and see what works best for your project.

Crate Engines

If you pull the trigger on a crate engine, you will definitely spend a few more bucks than on a junkyard rebuild project but it is a guaranteed engine with a bit more horsepower in most cases. Factory-fresh versions are available from all of the Big Three manufacturers, and numerous crate

The joy of a crate engine is cracking open the wooden crate to see a mostly complete power plant, ready for installation. Sometimes it's not quite that easy, but crate engines certainly simplify the engine swap process. Items such as the oil pan, exhaust, and wiring still need to be addressed but this LS3 is essentially ready to run.

Ford and Mopar enthusiasts have sources for crate engines as well, and it always requires extensive measuring to determine whether or not it will physically fit in the application. Ford and Mopar engines are wider than most modern GM engines, so they provide another series of challenges.

Modern Hemi Applications

5.7-liter
Iron block, aluminum heads, 340–399 hp
2003–present Dodge Ram
2004–present Dodge Durango
2005–present Chrysler 300C
2005–2008 Dodge Magnum R/T
2006–present Dodge Charger R/T
2005–present Jeep Grand Cherokee

2006–2010 Jeep Commander
2007–2009 Chrysler Aspen
2009–present Dodge Challenger R/T

6.1-liter
Iron block, aluminum heads, 425 hp
2005–2010 Chrysler 300C SRT-8
2005–2008 Dodge Magnum SRT-8

2006–2010 Dodge Charger SRT-8
2006–2010 Jeep Grand Cherokee
  SRT-8
2008–2010 Dodge Challenger SRT-8

6.4 (aka 392)
Iron block, aluminum heads, 475 hp
2011–present SRT-8 vehicles

engine suppliers, including Mast Motorsports, offer upgraded versions with big power gains.

Engine Upgrades

The rationale for swapping a modern engine into a Pro Touring car is to take advantage of the weight savings, reliability, and performance of today's power plants. Because it's a car guy's nature to make things better, lighter, and faster, upgrading the engine is a no-brainer. Small details to help the engine breathe easier and swallow a bit more fuel can wake up any modern engine. The to-do list generally consists of headers, free-flowing exhaust, a larger throttle body, and possibly larger fuel injectors. These bolt-on items can add a noticeable amount of horsepower to the already-powerful engine by increasing throttle response and taking advantage of the engine's efficiency.

So, the engine has crested the 400-hp mark and you're hungry for more? That means you have to dig

If you want the advantages of a highly efficient engine but don't want to deal with fuel injection, there are plenty of components to perform a carburetor swap. It seems as if you're going backward but it definitely simplifies the wiring harness and makes it easier for folks who have previously dealt with carburetors.

a little deeper into your wallet. For many builds, a more aggressive camshaft and accompanying valvetrain components can add big-time horsepower and provide the classic muscle car sound of a choppy idle. A camshaft, lifter, valvespring, and rocker arm swap costs around $2,000 for an LS-based engine; it's money well spent as long as the camshaft specs line up with the engine's capabilities. It's easy to reach for the biggest camshaft on the shelf but that is rarely

applicable to a street application, so keep it simple and make sure the engine can keep up. Details such as compression ratio, max RPM, vehicle weight, and rear-end gear are considered when selecting the correct camshaft, so keep these in mind when making your decision.

Cylinder heads are another place to gain a lot of power but many modern engines feature outstanding flow numbers from the factory. In other words, it takes a lot of effort to make the cylinder heads the weakest link in the engine combination. That means you can throw a bunch of fuel and air to it, and the cylinder heads aren't going to hold you back. If you're dealing with an old-school small-block or big-block, a set of aftermarket aluminum cylinder heads are a welcome addition to get the most out of the combination in terms of horsepower gains and weight savings.

Induction has always been a go-to area for muscle car enthusiasts. Years ago, the idea was to install a bigger carburetor and an aluminum intake manifold. Truth be told, these modifications may have been good for 10 or 15 hp on a stock engine; still, it was the thing to do. With the

Even if you keep the modern engine completely stock, you want a custom exhaust with high-performance mufflers. Not only do these Borla mufflers offer added performance, they also provide an awesome tone from the tailpipes. Most Pro Touring builds feature a 3-inch exhaust system constructed from stainless steel.

If you've maxed out the power output without tapping into the engine's internals, the camshaft is the first place to go. It's a pretty serious step but it can provide some big-time horsepower gains and an aggressive idle. Many companies offer aftermarket camshafts and valvetrain accessories to upgrade a modern engine.

Power adders are popular with all forms of high-performance vehicles. Although nitrous oxide and turbochargers are very popular in the drag racing scene, the most practical power adder in the Pro Touring world is the supercharger. It offers instant throttle response, and it's always there.

efficiency of GM's LS engine, Ford's mod motor, and Chrysler's modern Hemi, induction modifications are a bit different. The goal is still to allow more air and fuel to enter the engine, with many ways to go about it.

Most stock intake manifolds are capable of supporting lots of power; sometimes a modification is simply a matter of aesthetics. For instance, Mac Martin's 1969 Camaro has a GM Performance Parts LS3 engine under the hood, but instead of the stock composite intake manifold, it features an aluminum single-plane intake topped with a carburetor. Why would you throw away the fuel injection in favor of ancient technology? Simplicity is the number-one reason, and the fact that it looks cool in combination with the stock-style air cleaner was a good enough excuse to rewind technology.

Power adders are very popular in modern high-performance cars, and for good reason. They provide an extra boost in horsepower without internally modifying the engine. Power adders are the ultimate "bolt-on" modification but they're not cheap and they are not generally used in Pro Touring applications. Nitrous oxide, superchargers, and turbochargers are great eye candy, and certainly make more horse-

power, but none of these options makes for quicker lap times or better handling. If anything, the additional horsepower and an eager right foot may create a lot of tire spin, which is never a good thing. In most cases, you can get a reliable 500 hp out of a naturally aspirated late-model engine without breaking the bank, but the sky is the limit when you throw a power adder in the mix.

Making the Swap

You've decided to swap to a modern engine and you're ready for the next move. Depending on your application and your engine selection, it may be as simple as flipping through your favorite speed parts catalog and picking out the right components. Oil pans are almost always on the

parts list, as most stock pans do not clear the factory crossmember in most muscle car applications. In the case of LS engines, many people used an H2 Hummer oil pan in previous years, but you can now buy an aftermarket GM or Holley oil pan that is built specifically for muscle cars.

Unless you plan on running the stock exhaust manifolds, you need some headers to fit your car. Long-tube headers are suggested in most cases because they let the engine breathe, especially when combined with a large-diameter exhaust and free-flowing mufflers. Engine swap headers are available for many engine swap setups but odd combinations may require custom fabricated headers. Expect to pay well into the thousands for custom headers, but if that's you're only option, it's best to consider those costs before digging too deeply into an oddball engine swap.

An LS swap into a first-generation Camaro is relatively easy but a mod motor swap into a Ford Maverick may not yield the same sort of painless result because of the extent of the modifications to make it fit.

The most obvious components of an engine swap are the engine mounts. To install a modern power plant into a muscle car means that the

When it's time to slide the engine and transmission into place, there's no better feeling than seeing all of the swap-specific components work together. The engine mounts and oil pan will be your first victories, and then you have to tackle the transmission mount and headers.

There was a time when all engine-swapped cars required custom-built headers that cost well into the thousands of dollars. Now you can buy headers that are ready to bolt onto the specific combination. They're still fairly expensive but you're saving lots of time and money, and they look cool!

engine mounts most likely need to be relocated for proper fitment. Solid mounts are very simple to fabricate but they are not suggested for a street car. Even though you don't want a lot of flex from the engine and transmission, it's best to avoid solid mounting in most cases. A store-bought motor mount kit is ultimately quicker and easier than building your own.

Although it doesn't seem like a normal part of the engine swap routine, you must also consider upgrading the cooling system. Using the LS engine as an example, it has both water outlets on the passenger's side of the car, whereas most old-school small-block and big-block engines use a radiator with the upper outlet on the driver's side and the lower outlet on the passenger's side. This requires a radiator with both inlets on the passenger's side. A number of options are available for muscle car applications, all of which feature aluminum construction, which is great for cooling and weight savings.

It's also important to consider the accessory drive, as it varies from engine to engine and could cause a major headache if you try to use

One of the most important aspects of the engine swapping process are the engine mounts. Detroit Speed manufactures mounts that feature a steel A-frame that bolts to the crossmember, an aluminum plate that bolts to the engine block, and a rubber isolator that fits between the two.

original brackets and pulleys. A good pulley system, such as the Vintage Air Front Runner, includes items such as the water pump, A/C compressor, alternator, and more, so don't let the price scare you away.

Wiring is another aspect to consider when performing an engine swap. The easiest option is to buy a ready-made wiring harness kit. Companies can build the harness to your exact needs and save you a lot of time and effort. Tracing all of those wires, and then finding which ones are necessary and unnecessary, may be fun to some people, but to most of us it's torture. Anything to make engine swap wiring easier gets a warm welcome.

This is why you pay the big bucks for high-quality headers: You want them to fit perfectly in that extremely small amount of real estate between the engine, frame rails, firewall, engine mounts, starter, and steering linkage. Cheap headers never fit correctly, and cause more headaches in the long run.

Water inlet and outlet locations determine the need for a new radiator in most engine swaps. For the popular LS engine swap, both the upper and lower radiator hoses are located on the passenger's side of the car. Always use an aluminum radiator for any high-performance build.

Transmission

A big part of the Pro Touring movement is the ability to hop into your muscle car and drive it a long distance without fear of overheating or breaking parts. Overdrive transmissions have certainly helped the cause by providing low-RPM cruising. Whether you choose an automatic or manual transmission, you can expect to find plenty of choices for turning the horsepower into motivation. Much the same as modern engine swaps, these late-model transmissions require a bit of work to fit them into a classic muscle car platform.

The ideal setup for a Pro Touring application is a manual overdrive transmission with a strong clutch and a short-throw shifter. Managing three pedals, a steering wheel, and a shifter is quite the task, but it's part of the fun of slinging an old car around a racing course. If the machine spends more time on the street than on the racing course, and you'd rather let the transmission do all the work, there is no shame in choosing an automatic. Automatic transmissions are perfectly fine for regular driving but they just don't

Fitting a modern transmission into a classic car is quite the task, even if you plan to keep an old-style engine combination. Late-model transmissions are longer, wider, and heavier than older transmissions, so be prepared for some fabrication and heavy lifting to make it work.

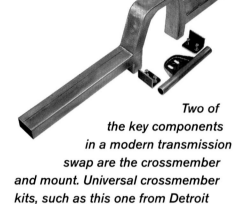

Two of the key components in a modern transmission swap are the crossmember and mount. Universal crossmember kits, such as this one from Detroit Speed, allow you to determine the appropriate location for the transmission and then modify the crossmember and mount to fit.

have the same effectiveness on the race course. Most hardcore Pro Touring cars have a manual transmission.

Regardless of your transmission choice, you will likely run into some fitment issues if you use a modern transmission. Most newer transmissions are much larger than transmissions from the 1960s and 1970s. That means you have to do some cutting, fabricating, and welding to make sure the transmission fits correctly in the tunnel. A custom transmission crossmember is also necessary to mount

the transmission to the chassis. Moving farther back, you also need a custom driveshaft, as the longer transmission generally necessitates a shorter driveshaft.

As you can see, almost every component needs attention to make all of the pieces work in harmony. Eventually you run out of things to upgrade, and that's when you start on your second Pro Touring project car!

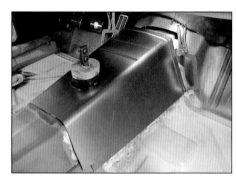

Because of the drastic size difference between modern manual and automatic transmissions, you may need to reshape the transmission tunnel. This is especially the case in builds that use half-height subframe bushings, as they effectively raise the engine and drivetrain. Either way, a new hole for the shifter must be cut.

The accessory drive on modern engines is quite different from that on old engines. Most new engines must power the alternator, water pump, power steering pump, and A/C compressor, and a nicely packaged accessory drive system makes for a much cleaner appearance. This is a Vintage Air Front Runner kit.

Project: Engine Installation

1 An engine swap requires a number of parts and tools, and it's very convenient to lay them out on a large table. Here are the oil pan and accessories, engine mounts, starter, bellhousing, and headers.

2 The first step is to lift the engine using a hoist. If you plan to perform any modifications to the engine, now is the time to put it on an engine stand.

3 The original oil pan that comes with an LS3 out of the crate is not applicable for most Pro Touring builds because it features a very large sump that does not clear the crossmember.

4 If you're dealing with a junkyard engine or a "take out" engine from another car, this is a great time to drain the oil. Remove the original bolts from the cast-aluminum oil pan, and lower it from the engine.

5 LS engines feature a windage tray, which bolts to the block with 10 nuts. The new oil pan requires a new windage tray, so remove the old one and bolt the new one into place.

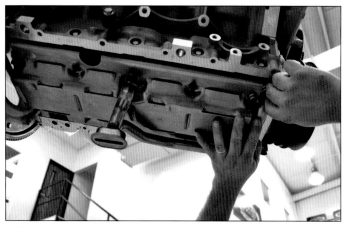

6 The oil-pickup tube bolts into place at the front of the engine and features a mounting bracket on the center windage tray stud on the passenger's side of the engine.

7 Use the GM oil pan gasket (PN 12612350) when replacing the oil pan. Always spread a small amount of high-temperature RTV on gasket surfaces. Luckily, modern engines with cast-aluminum oil pans aren't nearly as susceptible to oil leaks as older engines with stamped-steel pans.

8 Bolt the new pan (PN 12624617) into place. This pan fits many muscle car applications because of the size and location of the sump. This oil pan is original equipment for 2005–2013 Corvettes with LS2 and LS3 engines and fits GM muscle cars perfectly. Aftermarket pans are available through Holley and Mast Motorsports.

9 With the LS3 engine ready for installation, the next step involves bolting the steel engine mounts to the crossmember. Hand-tighten the three bolts to allow some wiggle room.

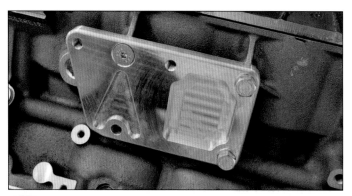

10 Next are the aluminum plates that bolt to the block. The countersunk Allen-head bolt must be flush against the aluminum plate, as the rubber isolator mounts on top of it.

11 The aluminum plate is threaded; the three retaining bolts for the rubber isolator are threaded into place and tightened.

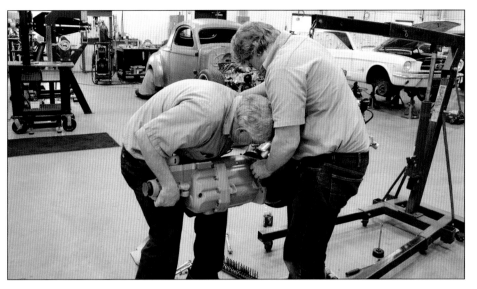

12 Now the bellhousing and transmission can be installed. In this case, the transmission is there for mock-up purposes, but in most situations this is the time to install the flywheel, clutch, and pressure plate.

13 The moment of truth is when the engine and transmission are hoisted into the air and poked into the engine bay. This is when an engine leveler really comes in handy.

14 Engine and transmission installation is a team sport: You need one person underneath to make sure the transmission fits correctly, one person operating the hoist, and a third person to check for clearance issues.

15 *A sigh of relief can be heard throughout the neighborhood when the engine is resting on the mounts and the hoist can be removed. Your muscle car now has an LS engine mounted in it!*

16 *For this build, Detroit Speed used a set of its stainless steel headers, which feature 1⅞–inch primary tubes and 3-inch collectors. The headers are equipped with bungs for oxygen sensors, so they're ready to plug into the aftermarket ECM.*

17 *With the front sheet metal removed from this Camaro, it's a great time to install the headers. This installation is usually a bit more challenging when the fenders, inner fenders, and hood are in the way.*

18 *Detroit Speed's headers are designed to fit with its hydroformed subframe kits, which utilize rack-and-pinion steering. A gap between the number-3 and number-5 primary tubes offers the perfect location for the steering shaft.*

19 *After the front sheet metal and engine accessories are installed, the LS3 engine looks right at home under the hood of Mac Martin's 1969 Camaro. In this case, the LS3 is now topped with a carburetor, and an original-style air cleaner mates up to the cowl induction hood.*

WIRING AND PLUMBING

Anyone who has built a car from the ground up can tell you that the big stuff is easy and the small stuff is the biggest headache. Suspension upgrades are usually straightforward, and you really feel as if you're making great progress with those types of installations. On the other hand, wiring and plumbing can sometimes feel like a never-ending process, and it doesn't provide the same sort of instant gratification that a bigger modification can provide. Just as with building a house, the walls go up quickly and the small details take the longest to complete.

The house example also puts the importance of wiring and plumbing into perspective. If something should go awry in the wiring or plumbing of your house, you may have to do some serious surgery to access it. Cutting through the wall of a brand-new house to access a faulty wiring connection, or cutting a hole in the floor to access plumbing components is sort of like tearing into a completed Pro Touring car because you cut corners on the wiring harness or plumbing system. It's not the smart thing to do. So while the car is torn to pieces, get the wiring harness straightened out and replace all of the lines, fittings, and hoses to make sure you don't end up with gremlins shortly after your car is completed.

The ideal time to install a new body wiring harness is when the engine and the interior are out of the

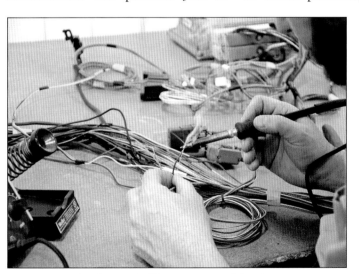

The days of having to build your own wiring harness are long gone, thanks to the tremendous support of the automotive aftermarket. Instead of piecing the wires together to form a substantial harness, you can now buy tailor-made harnesses built to your specifications.

Wiring can be a bit intimidating because regardless of how simple your car may seem, it still takes a lot of wires to power it. For a Pro Touring build that utilizes a late-model engine, air conditioning, and other modern treatments, you can expect to see a lot more wires.

An empty dash is a great starting point for a complete rewiring project. This allows you to start from scratch and wire each component, instead of having the entire harness and all of the components in the way.

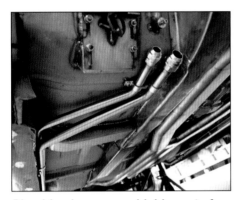

Plumbing is an unavoidable part of building any high-performance car. Generally, stock plumbing is not sufficient for Pro Touring builds, so fuel systems, brake systems, and oil systems must be addressed. This stainless steel plumbing is part of a dry sump oiling system.

car. This allows you to access all of the connection points easily, and it allows you to hide the wires appropriately. As for plumbing, new lines and hoses can be installed at any time but it's always easiest to install these items after the suspension system is installed. Then you can work around all of the suspension components, instead of assuming the lines don't interfere with moving parts on the car.

As boring and frustrating as it may be, wiring and plumbing work is necessary in your Pro Tour build, especially when you consider swapping in a modern engine and conveniences such as air conditioning, stereo, and so on. Fuel systems, dry sump oiling systems, cooling systems, and other components require a great deal of effort when it comes to plumbing a Pro Touring car. It's all part of the process. Get ready to dig a little deeper and learn about the final details of wiring and plumbing to wrap up a big project.

Power Source

Powering a Pro Touring car is a tough job. Your charging system needs to support an engine control module (ECM) and a number of accessories just to make the car functional. That's not including the creature comforts we all enjoy. Batteries seem like no-brainer territory but you need more than your basic parts store battery to power all of those electrical components. Optima is the top choice in the high-performance battery market, and that is Detroit Speed's choice in all of its builds.

On the subject of batteries, you need to know how and where to mount one in your car. Batteries are heavy; it's best to place it toward the rear of the car and position it as low as possible, even if it means cutting the trunk pan to make a recessed pocket for it. A number of lightweight batteries on the market help shed a few unwanted pounds but it's hard to compare to the reliability of an Optima high-performance absorbent glass mat (AGM) battery.

A battery hold-down is advised in all types of builds, but especially in a Pro Touring atmosphere, where the car experiences lots of G-forces from hard acceleration, hard braking, and hard cornering. The battery hold-down is usually very basic; still, it's an opportunity to add a bit of personality to the build. Billet aluminum battery mounts are available, but if you have some metal fabrication skills, making your own battery hold-down will certainly add to the car's cool factor.

The power source is a very important part of a car's electrical system. In most Pro Touring cars, the battery is relocated to the rear of the car for better weight distribution, and held in place with an aluminum hold-down bracket. AGM batteries, such as this Optima, are suggested for the high amount of voltage needed to power a modern engine.

Keeping the battery charged is the alternator's job, and it's very important when the engine management is dependent on a steady flow of electricity. A voltage drop can cause some major issues with the ECM, but a heavy-duty GM 145-amp alternator should provide sufficient charging power.

When you move a battery away from the front of the car, it takes a bit more juice to power the system. Detroit Speed suggests using 2-gauge-or-larger battery cables to provide sufficient voltage to the electrical system. In addition, notice the bulkheads used here, which are the suggested way to pass the power source through a floorpan or firewall.

Alternator wiring is straightforward in most cases. For old-school small-blocks, a "one-wire" alternator runs from a single 12-volt source. Newer GM engines feature a plug and a single wire. Yet again, a simple design, so you'd have to try pretty hard to get the wires mixed up.

The long distance between the battery and crucial items such as the ECM and starter mandates large battery cables (2 gauge or larger) to adequately transfer the power. Wire that's too small or an insufficient battery could result in reduced cranking power, especially on a hot day. Detroit Speed always uses bulkheads to safely pass a 12-volt power cable through a panel, such as a firewall or floorpan. This bulkhead allows for multiple connections to the main hot wire and ground wire. This makes for simple wire routing and a safe wiring system.

When it comes to keeping the power source charged, you need a heavy-duty alternator, especially if you plan to use a modern fuel-injected engine. Providing power to individual coil packs, fuel pumps, sensors, and the regular wiring harness is a tough job for any charging system.

For a Pro Touring build, a 100-amp alternator is the minimum, but even a stock replacement GM alternator for most LS engine applications features 105 amps. You can also get a stock replacement 145-amp alternator, which is a heavy-duty application for a truck. If you'd rather go the aftermarket route, plenty of companies, such as Powermaster, build custom alternators with amp ratings as high as 350. Your build is unlikely to need such an extremely powerful alternator, so most Pro Touring enthusiasts should aim for a 150-amp alternator to help the charging system keep up.

Wiring Harness

Every car, no matter how stripped down it was from the factory, has a wiring harness. It can be as simple as the necessary engine wiring along with a few wires to power the lights, or it can consist of hundreds of wires to power a late-model engine, a stereo system, and whatever else you can dream up. Even though it can be complicated and somewhat expensive, wiring is not something to take lightly. Cutting corners on a car's wiring always results in a "side of the road" experience. Take the time to do it right, and you'll kiss those dreaded wiring gremlins good-bye.

Unless you're a wiring black belt, and enjoy a challenge, I suggest purchasing an aftermarket wiring harness. Most companies, such as American Autowire, can build a custom harness for your vehicle and work in the necessary wiring for specific accessories. The greatest part of a high-quality aftermarket wiring harness is that the correct connectors are already in place; all you have to do is read the labels to figure out where the wires belong. Simplifying

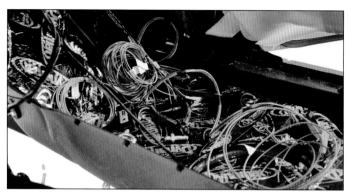

It's easy to become confused when turning this bundle of wires into an electrical system is on your agenda. Luckily, most wiring harnesses (even custom-built systems) feature labeled and color-coded wires to make it easy to sort out the wires. It's still a time-intensive process but the wiring harness companies certainly make it easier.

Most Pro Touring build candidates are nearing 50 years of age, so even if the lights and accessories are still in working order, it's best to replace the wiring harness. The harness for the lights is fairly straightforward, so it's certainly worth the time and effort to avoid an intermittent problem.

the wiring process has helped a lot of enthusiasts make easy work of revamping their vehicle's electrical system.

Many muscle cars and pony cars had rough lives throughout 40-plus years on the road. More accurately, the years on the road weren't that rough but the years in some guy's garage did a lot of damage. And I'm not just talking about the years of storage. I'm referring to the relentless hacking that car guys perform

to make their cars cooler or faster. Things have gotten a lot better, but the 1960s, 1970s, and 1980s were rough on muscle cars because folks didn't have the same resources we now enjoy. Gearheads didn't hesitate to strip a car's wiring harness to the bare minimum or wire in some sort of trendy accessory. This lack of preservation made for some ridiculously butchered wiring harnesses.

Luckily, the demand for replacement harnesses created a whole new

segment of the automotive aftermarket, which made it easy for restorers and hot rodders to rewire their cars without being a licensed electrician. If not for aftermarket wiring harnesses, this chapter would be a lot more complicated. I cover the basics of the body wiring harness and then go into detail about the engine wiring harness to illustrate the necessary wires and connectors to make a modern engine come to life when you turn the ignition switch.

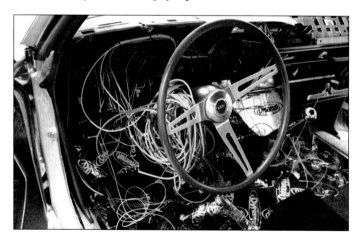

Dash wiring gets messy, even for the best in the business. Wires for the ignition switch, lights, stock gauges, auxiliary gauges, stereo system, air conditioning, and more is tucked behind the dash, where you find the largest quantity of wires.

After all items are wired and installed, the finished product shows no signs of its previous mess. It's quite a task to keep a wiring harness neat and tidy but patience is the key to making it happen.

Body and Dash Wiring Harness

Every car has one; it's just a matter of how many accessories it powers. Every car has external and internal lights but the real complications come into play when you add creature comforts, such as air conditioning, power windows, and stereo systems. Obviously, these things are not totally necessary to drive the car but if you're spending the money to build it, you may as well make it comfortable! Unless you're building an all-out race car, these comforts do not affect the performance of your car in a negative way.

Most standard wiring harnesses feature at least 12 circuits, accommodating a number of possible accessories. At least five of those circuits are devoted to external lighting, and you can expect to see the other circuits occupied by a horn, coil, radio, and the like. The most popular aftermarket wiring harnesses feature an 18-circuit design, adding provisions for electric fuel pumps, electric fan(s), air conditioning, and more.

The main fuse block feeds power to all of the harnesses within the car. The dash harness is included in

This is an example of a stock-style GM fuse block, complete with glass-tube–type fuses. Many modern wiring harnesses feature an updated fuse block with new blade-type fuses and additional circuits that offer the provisions to wire-in accessories that may not have been available in the 1960s.

A major relief when using an aftermarket wiring harness is that you're starting from scratch with brand-new color-coded and labeled wires. It doesn't get much easier than that, unless, of course, you have a friend who enjoys wiring more than you do.

that group, and sends power to the gauges, interior lights, radio, heat and air conditioning systems, and other accessories. The dash harness is always a frustrating install because it generally requires you to do most of the work on your back. Under-dash work isn't fun but it's a key to building a solid car that provides thousands of worry-free miles, no matter how hard you thrash on it.

Even with basic wiring harnesses,

you can expect to find color-coded wires, appropriate connectors, and thorough instructions. Companies such as American Autowire, Painless Performance, and others have made wiring classic cars, hot rods, and Pro Touring cars much easier to tackle. It still takes time and patience but the convenience of turning the switch to activate the ignition, fuel system, ECM, and all of the other accessories is certainly worth the effort.

Wiring to the gauges can vary greatly, depending on your preference to use stock-style gauges or outfit your car with custom gauges. Either way, you're looking at some in-depth wiring to monitor the engine's vital signs.

It's always suggested to take advantage of any component that you can wire from outside the vehicle. You'll spend plenty of time under the dash but if you can get started on the workbench, it'll save you some back pain at the end of the day.

Engine Swap Harness

As you learned in Chapter 8, swapping a modern engine into a muscle car is straightforward, as long as you have the necessary parts. Without these parts, it's a major headache, as you'd be fighting to fabricate mounts, find the right oil pan, build a set of headers, and the list goes on. When all of the parts are laid out in front of you, it's just a matter of bolting it all together.

The same can be said for the engine wiring harness. If you want to use a junkyard harness, you can make it work but it's going to be labor intensive, even if you know what you're doing. Some folks have a knack for wiring but a large percentage would rather shell out a few more dollars to simplify their wiring experience and make sure it works on the first go-round.

Engine wiring harnesses can be expensive but most of them are tailored to your specific combination, so it's a bit more involved than throwing a bundle of wires into a box

and mailing it to your house. A custom engine wiring harness can generally be installed in a short period of time, if the harness is complete and all of the sensors and plugs are installed on the engine. The plugs are different enough to easily distinguish one from another, so once all sensors are in place, it's a matter of plugging them together and moving on to the next one. A number of sensors feed signals to the ECM, so if any sensors are removed from the engine, the ECM must be programmed accordingly. Otherwise, the ECM assumes that the sensor is faulty, which can cause major problems. A custom-tuned ECM, along with a tailored engine wiring harness, is something a novice can easily install but it's not something you could modify on your own.

Also remember that modern engine swaps usually include a modern transmission. If you run a manual transmission, there aren't any wires to worry about, aside from the speedometer hookups and reverse lights. However, if you use a modern (General Motors, Ford, or Mopar) automatic transmission you

must also use an ECM to power the electronic functions of the transmission. Companies such as Compushift produce aftermarket modules to control modern transmissions. The Compushift module is fully programmable and user-friendly, making it easy to modify the original transmission settings. This controls the shift points, converter lock-up, and other electronically controlled features of most modern transmissions.

Even though an aftermarket engine wiring harness typically has the unnecessary wires removed from the system, you're still dealing with quite a bundle of wires that lead to a rather unattractive ECM. It's always nice to hide the ECM somewhere beneath the dash, and route the wires as neatly as possible, so that the engine bay is tidy. A modern engine has a lot more wires, hoses, and fittings than an old-school engine, so making all of these items look presentable is often a great challenge. Every car is different, so take the time to find good hiding spots for the ECM and bundles of wires.

The ECM can generally be placed in the glove box or somewhere inside

Engine swaps require a lot of additional wiring but the ECM is the brain behind the madness. It handles every major function of the engine, from the ignition to the fuel system and necessary sensors. A stock ECM must be reprogrammed when used in a vintage car because of the reduced number of accessories on an engine swap into an older vehicle.

Whether you plan to run a stock-style ECM (shown) or an aftermarket ECM, it needs voltage to operate, and feeds a big bundle of wires with signals to operate the engine. This very important aspect of the engine wiring needs to be mounted out of harm's way.

Modern automatic transmissions feature a control module to operate all transmission functions. In most cases, an aftermarket transmission controller, such as a Compushift unit, offers upgraded transmission functions while retaining the original transmission connector.

the car or engine bay. The enemy of the ECM is heat and electrical interference, so if you're running an aftermarket ignition box, or a high-powered electronic distributor, be sure to keep the ECM a safe distance away. Also keep the ECM away from extreme heat but keep it easily accessible for quick removal in the case of maintenance, tuning or repair.

It's important to note that the engine swap wiring harness is a separate unit from the car's main harness. Many companies, such as American Autowire, offer wiring harnesses for classic cars, which feature additional circuits to make engine swaps and other accessories possible. An engine swap harness reduces the original wiring diagram to get rid of the features on most modern engines, and this is generally customizable to meet your needs.

Mast Motorsports is one of the leaders in engine swap harnesses; they also provide an upgraded ECM to complete the package. If you're using an original-style ECM, it is important to use the ECM that is specific to the engine, and have it re-programmed to work with the vehicle and the new wiring harness. Do not mix and match stock ECMs as they are specific to each engine and transmission setup.

Plumbing

Similar to wiring, a vehicle's plumbing is quite important, and it's often forgotten until the last minute. Even if it's done well, it never gets any attention because it's hidden beneath layers of fancy parts, shiny paint, and a big engine. Taking the time to do it right, even though it may never be seen, is what makes plumbing so difficult to execute.

Plumbing varies greatly depending on application. A moderate build may use a slightly upgraded plumbing system, whereas a more radical build uses larger lines at every available opportunity. Braided stainless steel lines and AN fittings are commonplace in most Pro Touring builds.

Plumbing, much like many other aspects of Pro Touring cars, is far more complicated than a stock muscle car setup. Normally, a stock muscle car only needs fuel lines and brake lines plumbed from front to rear. Rubber hoses make up the rest of the fluid systems, such as the coolant system and power steering system. With a high-performance build, it's very popular to upgrade the plumbing system from hard steel lines and rubber hoses to high-performance, braided AN lines and fittings.

AN Lines and Fittings

You may have heard of AN lines but you may not have a clear understanding of why they're better than regular steel lines and rubber hoses. The name "AN" is an abbreviation for Army/Navy, which is where this system of lines and fittings was created. It's a very simple system but people are often confused because American car builders are so accustomed to the SAE system.

Special tools come in handy when building a plumbing system. For rubber hoses and lines, this cutter makes for a quick and straight cut. If you're dealing with braided lines and AN fittings, you need a set of AN line wrenches. In addition, be sure to keep plenty of thread sealer on hand to keep the fittings from leaking.

AN fittings are based on 1/16-inch increments. For instance, a -4 AN line equates to a 4/16-inch hard line and a -8 AN line equates to an 8/16-inch line. It's a simple system, but these line sizes are not to be confused with the fitting sizes. Using the same examples of a -4 and -8 AN line, that would equate to a 7/16-20

Braided lines and AN fittings are used on high-performance cars, and they are the ideal setup for fuel lines, coolant lines, and oil lines. Custom hoses and fittings can be costly but they provide a perfect fit. When you're dealing with tight clearances, a perfect fit is worth the price.

AN fittings feature a special design that uses a tapered seat and a special straight thread, instead of tapered threads as on an NPT fitting. The AN system originated in the military, and it's quite simple, even though it doesn't cross over with any other type of automotive plumbing components.

It's easy to convert your Pro Touring car's fuel system to braided lines and AN fittings; most aftermarket fuel system components feature AN fittings out of the box. High-quality fuel pumps, fuel regulators, and fuel filters can be equipped with AN fittings for a worry-free plumbing system.

SAE thread and 3/4-16 SAE thread, respectively.

In addition to the different sizing lingo, AN lines and fittings feature a different flare angle (37 degrees), and a different thread type. The National Pipe Thread (NPT) fitting features a tapered thread that acts as a wedge when it is tightened. This wedge design generally does not consistently create a positive seal without the use of thread sealant. AN fittings feature straight thread, like a normal fastener, making a much tighter seal without the use of thread sealant. AN fittings tend to be a bit more attractive than NPT fittings, and give your car a race-ready appearance.

It is common to use adapters to convert NPT fittings to accept AN lines and vice versa, but it's generally more efficient to simply start from scratch with the AN system. Many automotive plumbing suppliers offer full product lines in AN sizing, from small oil lines to large coolant lines.

Fuel Lines

Originally, muscle cars came with a mechanical fuel pump and a mixture of hard steel lines and rubber hoses. Steel lines tend to corrode after years of neglect beneath a car. This rust can eventually create a leak or contaminate the fuel system. Even on stock rebuilds or lightly modified cars, you should replace the hard lines and all rubber hoses to ensure a solid and worry-free fuel system. For a Pro Touring build, you can take this one step further by using braided stainless steel lines (with Teflon inner liners) with AN fittings.

It's very important to choose the right style of hose for the application. For instance, a standard braided stainless steel hose only has a life expectancy of a few years when used as a fuel supply hose because of corrosion of the liner. Pro Touring cars, like many collector vehicles, do not see nearly as much use as daily drivers, and the days of no activity accelerate the corrosion of the liner. The best way to avoid this problem is to always use a high-quality braided hose with a Teflon liner, built to withstand the corrosive nature of today's fuel.

Speaking of which, ethanol-enriched gasoline plays a big part in premature fuel system failure. Just 10-percent ethanol added to gasoline has been proven to cause major

Braided stainless steel lines can be used to transport fuel but be sure to use lines that feature a Teflon liner to resist corrosion. Hard lines are connected to braided flex lines using a bulkhead (shown), complete with black AN fittings.

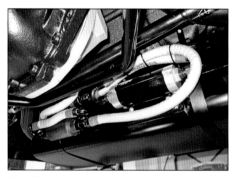

Pro Touring builds can utilize an in-tank (submerged) fuel pump, or you can use an inline (external) pump (shown). Inline pumps once had a bad reputation for overheating and eventually failing but units such as this Holley HP pump are built to withstand the abuse.

Regardless of your choice of a carburetor or fuel injection, you need a fuel pressure regulator. Electric pumps are highly efficient and unregulated, usually providing too much fuel to the engine. Generally, a vacuum signal from the engine determines how much fuel is sent to the return line.

A bank of toggle switches is cool in a race car but it generally doesn't offer the clean look that most folks want in a street car. A great solution is to use an original element of the car to hide auxiliary switches. This chrome cover in Detroit Speed's 1963 Chevy II test car is a prime example.

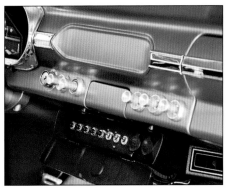

When the chrome cover is flipped down, a full set of switches, buttons, and ports is available. It's always important to position any auxiliary switches in an easy-to-reach location. Race cars usually have labels on or around the switches because it can be tough to remember the purpose of each switch when there are numerous switches on the same panel.

problems, especially if the car sits for extended periods of time. Try your best to find 100-percent gasoline when possible; it's the best fuel for any older vehicle.

If you choose to go with hard fuel lines, it's best to use stainless steel or aluminum lines because regular steel may suffer from rust and corrosion. Even then, you need some sort of flexible hose to connect the hard line to the engine. For this, you may use braided hose, as long as it is Teflon-lined.

Fuel Pump

Unlike stock muscle cars, Pro Touring builds generally feature an electric fuel pump, which is plumbed into the system by either mounting it inside the tank (with the sending unit) or mounting it externally. The advantage of an internal pump is that it is submerged in fuel, which keeps it cool. As for an external pump (sometimes referred to as an inline pump), it is mounted inline with the fuel supply lines, in the rear of the car.

Fuel flows through the pump, which then pushes fuel through to a fuel pressure regulator. Whether you run a carburetor or a fuel injection system, a fuel pressure regulator is a must. Aftermarket, and even stock, replacement fuel pumps create too much pressure for most engine applications. After the fuel pressure is regulated, the lines finally reach the engine.

On many modern fuel-injected engines, a fuel return line is required for proper fuel supply. It is important to note that stock fuel tanks and sending units generally do not have a return port. Only muscle cars equipped with smog equipment have a return port in the sending unit, but aftermarket sending units are available with the additional port needed for a return-style fuel system. Returnless fuel systems are also an option if you're using a stock tank and sending unit.

In the race car world, it is popular to wire the electric fuel pump to a toggle switch so that fuel supply can be halted at any given time.

Even though Pro Touring builds are race inspired, most enthusiasts don't want to clutter their dash with a bunch of toggle switches. The preferred method is to wire the fuel pump to be powered on when the ignition switch is in the on position.

It's advised to run the fuel pump wiring through a three-prong oil pressure switch so that the fuel pump kicks off when the engine is not running. A straight-wired fuel pump (without the pressure switch) could be a major safety hazard because there is no way to disable the fuel pump. Since the fuel pump is so far away from the source, it is important to use a five-pin relay so that the pump gets full voltage without overloading the switch.

Coolant Lines

Transferring coolant from the engine to the radiator is usually pretty straightforward. Most of us have always relied on the trusty rubber radiator hose and worm-style clamps for our coolant flow needs, which is by far the easiest method. The only difficult part of using rubber hoses is sneaking behind the counter at the local parts store to rummage through all the different hoses to find the right size, length, and bends.

Many companies sell custom radiator hose kits so you can convert from standard rubber hoses to the braided stainless steel look. These kits still feature a clamp but hide the adjustment screws in a stylish coupler. Hardcore racers use AN lines for coolant, which require custom bungs in the radiator and thermostat housing. Another option for stylish coolant lines is to use stainless steel round tubing to make the appropriate bends, and silicone couplers to attach to the engine and radiator. The stainless steel can then be polished for a chrome-like finish.

Coolant lines are often treated as off-the-shelf items from the parts store. On most cars, including Pro Touring builds, a standard set of radiator hoses is sufficient, but if you want a bit of race car flair you can always opt for AN fittings and braided lines. This requires custom bungs and fittings on the engine and radiator.

Project: Wiring Harness Installation

Wiring a modern engine, such as this supercharged LS engine, is generally a matter of plugging in the appropriate connectors. Custom wiring harnesses make the process even easier, as the ECM is already programmed to work with the engine combination.

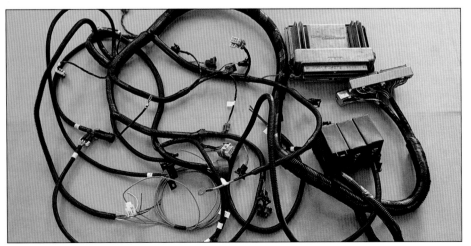

1 *This is a typical engine wiring harness for an LS engine that has been stripped down to the bare essentials. The ECM is reprogrammed to function with the minimal harness, and all of the connectors are in place and ready for installation.*

2 Before plugging in any of the connectors, take great care to route the wiring neatly. It's always best to tuck the wiring out of sight but also be careful that it is out of harm's way. In this instance, "harm's way" consists of heat and moving parts that could result in a wire failure.

3 Wiring for various sensors and senders is routed down the side of the engine block. In the case of an LS engine, each connector is a different shape, so it's easy to figure out where the wires should be connected, even if they are not labeled.

4 Fuel injector wiring is straightforward; the connectors can fit in only one orientation. You should have one connector per injector, totaling eight connectors.

5 Ignition wiring is also straightforward, with connectors for each coil. A total of eight coil pack connectors should attach to the individual coils.

6 The ECM uses signals from the engine's oxygen sensors to determine the appropriate air/fuel ratio. Generally oxygen sensors are threaded into bungs in the exhaust headers, and the connectors are plugged into the engine harness.

7 Aftermarket ECMs, such as this Mast Motorsports M-120 WBO2 unit, offer customized settings for high-performance engines. Mast Motorsports offers engine wiring harnesses complete with ECM to fit any modern LS engine application.

8 The camshaft position sensor is also connected to the engine harness. This sensor works in conjunction with a crankshaft position sensor to control the ignition timing. Gone are the days of rotating the distributor to advance or retard ignition timing!

9 Although it features many wires and connectors, it is possible to keep the engine wiring harness sanitary. The engine in Mac Martin's Camaro offers a simpler version of the wiring harness because it features a carburetor instead of fuel injection.

PRO TOURING CARS

Although most of this book concentrates on how to build your own Pro Touring car, it's always cool to see a few examples of nicely finished cars to get your creative juices flowing. Detroit Speed built all of the cars featured in this chapter and used an array of its high-performance products to make it happen. Popular GM platforms are covered, as well as early Ford Mustang platforms. Take a look at some of the coolest Pro Touring cars on the planet and get busy on your project car!

Mac's Camaro took on a whole new attitude with the Pro Touring treatment. The car's stance is low and offers ready-to-run looks, thanks to extra-wide Michelin rubber on all four corners. The beautiful silver paint job is part of the original COPO-style restoration.

1969 Camaro: COPO Conversion

In Chapter 4, a few pictures are featured of Mac Martin's 1969 Camaro in its restored configuration. Although very nicely done, the big-block engine, 4-speed transmission, and bare-bones suspension didn't allow this car to get out on the open road very often. The Pro Touring treatment certainly changed its attitude.

Many muscle car enthusiasts seek high-optioned cars with original packages, such as the Super Sport, Rally Sport, and so on. Others would rather cut up a base model car that has no real significance, and leave the high-dollar cars for the restorers to fight over. Mac Martin took a completely restored COPO Camaro clone to the folks at Detroit Speed for a complete Pro Touring makeover.

It might seem crazy to convert a COPO car, or even a well-executed COPO clone, into a Pro Touring machine but Mac Martin did just that with his 1969 Camaro. COPO stands for Central Office Production Order; it essentially means that the car was ordered with a special combination of options that didn't normally make it to the regular dealerships. In this case, the car featured a plain-Jane appearance but packed a 427-ci big-block, 4-speed manual transmission, and 12-bolt rear end. It was a hot combination in 1969, and these cars are still very desirable. A glitch in the serial numbers, however, can spell disaster for the car's value and authenticity.

When Mac Martin bought the Camaro, he paid for a documented and restored COPO, but when he decided to sell the car a few years later, he found out it wasn't a real-deal COPO. Because the car didn't have nearly as much value as he originally believed, he didn't mind giving it the Pro Touring treatment.

This type of build generally requires work that you wouldn't normally perform on a documented COPO, but since it was a clone, Mac pulled the trigger on a full-on Detroit Speed build. That means that instead of carefully loading his prized Camaro on and off of a trailer, he could drive cross-country with the convenience of air conditioning, fuel injection, overdrive, and a very capable suspension setup. Another high point of the Pro Touring conversion is the low stance, wide rubber, and awesome braking system, all aspects that provide a fun driving experience.

The crew at Detroit Speed took special care to protect the car's fresh silver paint job as well as the newly installed interior. Mac wanted to retain these elements but give the car the Detroit Speed Pro Touring treatment. So they wrapped up the body and started disassembling the car. Chassis modifications consisted of Detroit Speed subframe connectors and a mini-tub kit. While they were slicing the rear underpinnings of this pristine Camaro, they installed the necessary brackets (upper link pockets, Panhard bar bracket, coil-over bracket) to install a QUADRALink rear suspension. There is no doubt that Mac's Camaro is a purist's nightmare, but it's an incredible example of taking a stock muscle car and making it handle and perform like a new Corvette, maybe even better than a new Corvette.

LEFT: *Under the hood is a carbureted LS3 engine, which is equipped with Detroit Speed engine mounts and polished stainless steel headers, two items that made the modern engine swap quick and easy. The air cleaner is a custom piece that seals to the original cowl induction hood.* **RIGHT TOP:** *LS engine swaps generally require an aftermarket accessory drive system for a tidy appearance. Mac's Camaro features a Vintage Air front-runner system, which comes complete with polished serpentine pulleys. The cast-aluminum finish on the A/C compressor and alternator provides a nice contrast.* **RIGHT BOTTOM:** *The polished Holley cast-aluminum valve covers provide a bit of bright work and clean up the appearance of the coil packs. The stainless steel headers fit perfectly with the hydroformed subframe and steering shaft for the rack-and-pinion setup.*

For front suspension, the Camaro received a Detroit Speed hydroformed subframe kit, complete with tubular upper and lower control arms and a set of JRi aluminum body coil-over shocks with Detroit Speed tuned valving. The subframe kit also features a rack-and-pinion steering system, as well as a splined anti-roll bar for utmost stability in hard cornering. The front suspension system is tied together with Corvette-style spindles, which are hidden by Baer Claw Pro Plus disc brakes. This braking system features 14-inch slotted and cross-drilled rotors, and massive six-piston calipers with tons of clamping force.

The QUADRALink rear suspension features a parallel, unequal-length rear-suspension setup with sliding links that allow for ample articulation throughout the suspension cycle. In combination with another pair of JRi coil-overs, this rear suspension is ready for serious abuse. All of these components attach to a GM 12-bolt rear end, which is packed with a Detroit Truetrac differential, 3.73 gearset, and a pair of GM 30-spline axles. Rear braking is handled by a Baer Claw SS4 Plus system, which consists of 13-inch slotted and cross-drilled rotors and aluminum four-piston calipers. The rear brakes also feature an inter-nal parking brake, which is basically a drum brake inside the brake rotor hat.

Rolling stock on Mac's Camaro was originally 14 x 6–inch steel wheels with "dog dish" hubcaps and Goodyear Polyglas tires. The cool COPO look had to go because much larger tires and wheels would roll beneath the transformed Camaro. The Formula 43 Rad 6 front wheels measure 18 x 10 inches, wrapped in Michelin 275/35R18 rubber; the rears come in at 18 x 12 with matching Michelins, sized at 335/35R18. This size combination is something that Detroit Speed has documented and uses on a regular basis. With the aggressive stance and wide tire and wheel combination in mind, Detroit Speed knows that the rear-end housing must measure 54.75 inches from end to end. Backspacing on the rear wheels is 5.5 inches, providing a killer "deep dish" look, with more than 6 inches of spacing on the front side of the wheel.

For horsepower, Mac's Camaro relies on a GM Performance Parts LS3 crate engine. The LS3 is the choice for many Pro Touring enthusiasts because it features an all-aluminum construction and cranks out big-time horsepower out of the box. For this build, the Detroit

LEFT TOP: Inside, Mac's Camaro has a factory look, with all-black components, but the modern bucket seats and custom door panels add a bit of modern flair. The dash, steering wheel, and console are stock Camaro components, reused from the car's restoration. **LEFT BOTTOM:** Under the console lid is a controller for the Sony stereo system. All of the stereo equipment is hidden out of sight, and the original radio is still in place. The same can be said of the Vintage Air heat and A/C system, with hidden controls in the console and stock (nonfunctional) heater controls on the dash. **RIGHT:** Recaro bucket seats provide comfort and a modern element in the otherwise-stock interior. Behind the buckets is another pair of matching Recaro bucket seats. Details like this bring the car into the modern era without destroying its classic looks.

Speed crew kept it simple, retaining the stock LS3 long-block and performing only the modifications necessary to make it fit in the first-generation F-Body chassis. A Mast Motorsports LSX oil pan was the first modification, allowing the engine to fit properly. A set of Detroit Speed stainless steel headers provide a good-looking solution to the limited space for exhaust. The primary tubes in the headers measure 1⅞ inches and lead to a 3-inch stainless steel exhaust fit with Borla XR-1 race mufflers.

One major change to the LS3 engine comes in the way of induction. Normally it would feature a composite, low-profile intake manifold, but Mac's car has been converted to a carburetor. Although this is technically taking a step backward in technology, it's a cool way to utilize a stock-style air cleaner and greatly simplify the engine bay as well as the wiring harness. The fuel system is all Aeromotive components, from the Stealth fuel tank to the electric fuel pump. Braided lines with AN fittings run from front to rear on Mac's aptly equipped Camaro.

As for aesthetics, Mac's car didn't get much attention, mainly because it didn't need it. The car was a fresh restoration at the time of its Pro Touring transformation, so there was no need to ruin the pristine bodywork and paint. Detroit Speed protected the paint job throughout

Mac felt that it would be hard to improve on the bodylines and features of the 1969 Camaro, so the body and paint job remain stock. All trim, emblems, and handles are in place, but the Formula 43 Rad 6 wheels offer the right amount of race-inspired style for this Pro Touring creation.

LEFT: *Thanks to Detroit Speed deep tubs and QUADRALink rear suspension setup, the Camaro rolls on a pair of 335/35R18 tires out back. The wheels measure 18 x 12 inches with 5.5 inches of backspacing, and the total rear-end width is 54.75 inches. The front tires are 275/35R18 mounted to 18 x 10 wheels.* **ABOVE:** *Despite this car's very original starting point, it serves as a great example of transforming a stock muscle car into something that can perform well and provide a comfortable ride. The Detroit Speed treatment includes all the right ingredients to make a stock Camaro outperform a modern sports car.*

the build process, and took the same great care with the interior. However, they ditched the original bucket seats in favor of a pair of Recaro seats with matching contoured rear seats. Custom leather door panels add a bit of modern flavor to the classic Camaro interior, which retains the original dash, gauges, and steering wheel. Chuck Hanna at Hot Rod Interiors handled the stitch work.

A Hurst shifter pokes out of the original console and operates the Tremec TKO-600 5-speed manual transmission. Inside the console compartment is a Sony controller for the audio system, as well as the controls for the Vintage Air A/C and heat system.

The Detroit Speed treatment took four months, and Mac's first trial run with the car was the Hot Rod Power Tour, a week-long road trip that would truly test the car's new capabilities. With more than 500 hp on tap, mated to an overdrive transmission, the transformed 1969 Camaro offered great acceleration and comfortable highway RPM, something an original car could only dream about. The Power Tour is held in June; it provided a great opportunity for Mac to try out the air conditioning, and it proved to be the ultimate reliability test. As expected, it passed with flying colors and assured Mac that he'd gone in the right direction with this car. He can use it and abuse it on a regular basis, and still enjoy the beautiful lines and personality of a classic muscle car.

On the road, Mac's Camaro is comfortable and nimble, something that most stock muscle cars cannot claim. The ultimate test for this four-month build was the Hot Rod Power Tour, and the Camaro passed with flying colors.

1966 Mustang: Fastback Flyer

There's something to be said for an understated Pro Touring car. A clean white paint job and satin-black wheels do not provide an initial wow factor, but once this Boss-powered Fastback hits the track, people take notice. Subtle body modifications are tasteful and functional.

Although Detroit Speed got its start with the first-generation Camaro, it has grown immensely in the past few years. During this growth, new product lines have worked toward filling the gaps in the Pro Touring market. Detroit Speed jumped off the GM bandwagon to develop a complete suspension system for early Mustangs, and built an incredible Pro Touring 1966 Mustang in the process. Let's check out what makes it such a cool car.

The hunkered-down stance is the first thing most people notice. The tires and wheels fill the wheel openings perfectly, and there is plenty of contact patch on the front and rear tires. Yes, you can lower a Mustang and retain its original suspension design, and yes, you can widen the tubs to fit more tire out back. But Detroit Speed wanted Mustang enthusiasts to get the full Pro Touring treatment without tons of fabrication.

The solution is what Detroit Speed calls the Aluma-Frame, a bolt-in front suspension crossmember that gets rid of the original front suspension configuration altogether. An aluminum crossmember bolts to the top of the frame rail, providing mounts for the upper control arms and coil-overs. A lower crossmember bolts to the bottom side of the frame rails, providing mounts for the lower control arms, anti-roll bar, and rack-and-pinion. The crossmember also features provisions for several engine mount options: small-block Ford, big-block Ford

(FE), Ford mod motor, and even GM LS mounts if you're not a true Ford guy.

Originally, Mustangs featured a front suspension that used coil springs, which mounted on top of the upper control arm. This design does not lend itself well to the Pro Touring atmosphere; the Detroit Speed Aluma-Frame provides a more conventional coil-spring configuration and a completely new suspension geometry. This isn't just a Mustang II front suspension grafted to the front of an early Mustang; it's the real deal and it really works. Tubular control arms, JRi coil-over shocks, Detroit Speed spindles, and a splined anti-roll bar make up the highly functional front suspension, while a rack-and-pinion handles steering. One of the coolest aspects of the front suspension is Detroit Speed's patented Speed-LIGN caster/camber adjusters, which allow a wide range of adjustability without the use of shims.

The compact design of the Aluma-Frame front suspension system allows the use of 265/35R18 tires (mounted to a 18 x 9–inch wheel) on 1964–1968 Mustangs, and up to 295/35R18 tires (mounted to a 18 x 10.5–inch wheel) on 1969 and 1970 models. On the 1966 Mustang test car, Kyle opted for a set of 18 x 10–inch Formula 43 RAD S5 wheels, wrapped in 275/35R18 BFGoodrich g-Force Rival tires. As mentioned, 265 tires are usually the limit on the early Mustangs but the Detroit Speed crew rolled the fender lips

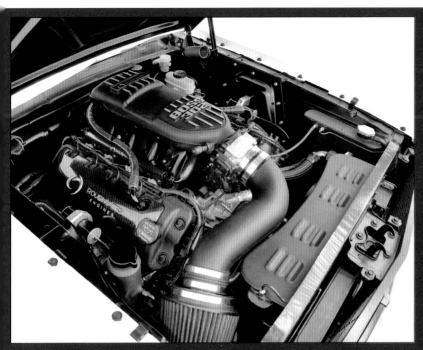

LEFT: *As you may have gathered, engine swaps in classic Mustangs (and any compact or midsize Ford platform) are quite challenging. Detroit Speed fixed this issue with a new front suspension system that gets rid of the bulky shock towers. The test car is powered by a Roush Yates–prepared Boss 302 mod motor, which has 5.0 liters in displacement.* **RIGHT TOP:** *As you can see, real estate was limited in the Mustang's engine bay, so the master cylinder is very close to the valve cover. Mod motors are very wide because of the dual overhead camshafts, so clearances are certainly tight. Despite the challenges of the physical size, the Coyote 5.0-liter engine is ideal for Pro Touring builds.* **RIGHT BOTTOM:** *A high-winding all-aluminum DOHC engine is just begging to be placed in a Pro Touring build. It cranks out more than 500 hp and weighs approximately 450 pounds, which greatly helps weight distribution. Behind the Boss 302 is a Tremec T-56 6-speed manual transmission.*

to gain a little more real estate. Out back, the Mustang features 315/30R18 Rivals, mounted to 18 x 11–inch wheels.

This tire and wheel combination is made possible by Detroit Speed's mini-tub kit, which features 2½-inch-wider inner tubs and small sections of boxed tubing to provide additional clearance around the rear frame rails. During the chassis revamping process, Detroit Speed also added subframe connectors and a roll cage to help the unibody structure hold up to the abuse of road racing and auto-cross racing.

The 1966 Mustang test car is equipped with Detroit Speed's QUADRALink rear suspension, which ditches the leaf springs in favor of a four-link system. Like the QUADRALink kits for other makes and models, this one features swivel-link technology on the upper and lower links to prevent binding as the suspension articulates. Add a set of custom-tuned JRi coil-over shocks and you have an unstoppable Pro Touring setup that outperforms those weak original leaf springs by a long shot.

The QUADRALink setup also features a splined anti-roll bar, an adjustable Panhard bar, and a strong upper crossmember that stiffens the rear frame section and provides mounting points for the coil-overs. All of these components attach to a Ford 9-inch rear end, which features a Detroit Truetrac differential, 4.56 gearset, and 31-spline axles for a bulletproof Pro Touring combination.

Braking on the test car consists of Baer equipment. A Baer 6R system is used on the front, utilizing 14-inch drilled and slotted rotors, with massive six-piston calipers to provide big-time clamping power. Out back is a Baer T4 system, using 13-inch drilled and slotted rotors with a high-performance four-piston caliper. The car has many race-inspired details, including proportioning valves mounted within the driver's reach for quick fine-tune adjustments to the brake bias.

For horsepower, a healthy Boss 302 Coyote engine consumes every square inch of the crowded engine bay. Even though it comes in at only 302 cubic inches (5.0 liters), it's a massive engine thanks to its DOHC design. The Boss 302 is a Ford Racing crate engine, and it's the perfect combination for a Pro Touring build. It has

LEFT: *Creature comforts are minimal inside the Mustang test car but this car sees a lot of track time, so it's an appropriate configuration. The gauge cluster, steering wheel, and seating arrangement are race-bred touches that see a lot of use. To say this interior is bare bones would be an understatement.* **MIDDLE:** *Early Mustangs had really cool sculpted inner door panels with a vinyl-wrapped insert. The Detroit Speed 1966 Mustang features louvered door-panel inserts with stock armrests and interior handles. The satin-black paint is simple but offers a great contrast to the white exterior.* **RIGHT:** *The T-56 6-speed is controlled with this custom shifter handle, which is straight out of a NASCAR vehicle. The Kevlar shifter boot is also race car material, but hey, those custom cup holders are street equipment, right? The two boxes in front of the shifter are the brain (ECM) for the Boss 302 engine.*

ABOVE: *The Detroit Speed Mustang test car rolls on BFGoodrich g-Force Rival tires, sized at 275/35R18 up front and 315/30R18 out back. The sticky rubber is mounted to a set of Formula 43 RAD S5 wheels, sized at 18 x 10 and 18 x 11 inches. Behind the satin-black spokes is a killer Baer 6R brake setup.* **LEFT:** *Although the purpose of racing seats is safety and weight reduction, these Sparco seats are quite comfortable. The harnesses and roll cage provide safety for the driver, while the racing seats conform to the driver to secure him or her in the event of a crash.*

high-revving capabilities, makes great horsepower, and features an all-aluminum construction. The Boss 302 cranks out 444 hp out of the box and weighs in at a mere 444 pounds, making this screamer a great performer.

The aluminum block is packed with forged internals, including forged pistons that create an 11.0:1 compression ratio. Aluminum cylinder heads feature a four-valve-per-cylinder design, with a total of four camshafts, making for great port efficiency. The Boss 302 also features variable valve timing, allowing it to have moderate timing during calm driving, and aggressive timing as RPM goes skyward.

On this application, the timing is locked to a particular setting for maximum horsepower. Induction consists of a single 80-mm throttle body feeding into a composite intake manifold. Roush Yates tuned the Boss 302, providing more than 100 hp over stock, and the healthy mod motor breathes through Detroit Speed stainless steel Coyote-swap headers and 3-inch exhaust, fit with Magnaflow mufflers. The airflow capabilities of these Coyote engines is what makes them so popular. Adjusting the timing and fuel delivery (along with a free-flowing intake and exhaust) allows this engine to make big-time power without digging too deeply into the engine.

Detroit Speed mated it to a T-56 manual transmission to put the power to the ground. Bowler Transmission prepared the 6-speed for serious abuse, packing the aluminum case with carbon fiber synchro rings, steel shift forks, and bulletproof input and output shafts.

In terms of appearance, the Detroit Speed Mustang test car is clean and simple with a white paint job and

A satin-black center stripe and a taillight panel are simple touches that give this 1966 Mustang a sinister look. The combination of Detroit Speed Aluma-Frame front suspension and QUADRALink rear suspension give the car a great stance, and provide a highly functional suspension system.

satin-black stripe on the hood. Satin black also covers the window trim, mirrors, and door handles to tie it all together. Body modifications are minimal and subtle, to retain the Mustang's original lines and proportions. The fastback body style is a favorite among Ford fans, so this car gets a lot of attention, especially when it hits the autocross course or road course.

Inside, it's all business, with minimal creature comforts. Two Sparco seats mount to the lowered and modified seat structure, and feature five-point safety harnesses. The test car doesn't have carpet, it doesn't have a stereo, and it doesn't have air conditioning. This Mustang is bred for racing, and does just that on a regular basis. The dash has been fitted with a selection of Auto Meter gauges to monitor the Boss 302 engine, while a removable Sparco steering wheel adds more race car flavor. A full roll cage protects the driver, and a pair of basic cup holders provides a small splash of convenience if a weekend cruise is on the schedule. The Spartan interior is just right for this race-inspired Pro Touring machine, but modern accessories and a full interior would certainly make for a more pleasant experience behind the wheel if you plan to make road trips and spend a lot of time on the highway.

Without question, the Detroit Speed 1966 Mustang offered the perfect platform to test an array of new products for one of the most popular pony cars. It's a welcome addition to the Pro Touring world, and it makes a classic Mustang perform as good as it looks.

TOP: *Although the Mustang test car has a lot of race-inspired details and a lack of creature comforts, it still hits the highway with ease and provides a comfortable ride. It's on the hardcore side of the Pro Touring spectrum but if you're serious about racing, this is the ideal setup.* **BOTTOM:** *Here's something you don't often see: a classic Ford Mustang with wide tires on all four corners. Generally, the original front suspension design is a major limiting factor for tire and wheel sizing, but the Aluma-Frame setup allowed for 275/35R18 tires on this build.*

1963 Chevy II: Size Matters

Pro Touring cars aren't often seen on the drag strip, but this photo was captured at LS Fest, an event that rewards LS-powered cars that can do it all. Detroit Speed is generally at the top of the food chain at this type of event, and the 1963 Chevy II test car is a fan favorite.

When it comes to the performance world, size matters. We always want big engines, big tires, and big brakes, but what happens when you cram all that big stuff into a car that's smaller than average? You have an all-out performer that carries around less weight than any of those Camaros, GTOs, and Mustangs. The Chevy II made its debut in 1962 as Chevy's second entry into the compact car market. The first entry was the Corvair but it was not a conventional car by General Motors (or any American auto manufacturer's) standards. The Chevy II offered a more conventional approach, with a unibody design and the trusty front engine/rear-wheel-drive setup that we all know and love.

Although Chevrolet produced these compact cars with the Super Sport package, it never intended to compete with its own performance cars at the time. The Chevy II sort of did that on its own; it was a lightweight car with enough room to fit a V-8 between the shock towers. From 1962 to 1967, the Chevy II remained a small car, but it grew tremendously in 1968 when it moved to the X-Body platform, a very close cousin to the F-Body platform. So, what's the big advantage of building a lightweight Pro Touring car, as opposed to building on the popular F-Body or A-Body platform? Lightweight cars accelerate quicker, stop faster, and turn better than their heavier brethren. It's as simple as that.

Detroit Speed owner Kyle Tucker loves the early Chevy II models and found the car that became his test car through a friend and coworker. Will Handzel, previous technical editor of *Hot Rod* magazine and engineer at General Motors, owned the Chevy II, having bought it at the Pomona Swap Meet many years before. When the car changed hands, Kyle knew that it was time to pull the trigger on the full Chevy II product line, and this car served as the perfect test car for the new components.

The car went under the knife to receive Detroit Speed mini-tubs so that a pair of 19 x 10–inch wheels and 295/35R19 rubber could fit comfortably. Chevy IIs are known for tight clearances for tires and wheels, so the mini-tubs made a huge difference. The unibody chassis also received a set of subframe connectors and a six-point roll cage to help stiffen the structure.

From there, the team developed and installed a QUADRALink kit for the compact Chevy II, using a four-link design that is similar to the design that works so well in the F-Body and other platforms. A Ford 9-inch rear-end housing is highly modified and is packed with a Detroit Truetrac differential, a 3.89:1 gearset, and Moser 31-spline axles. An adjustable Panhard bar and a splined anti-roll bar provide the right amount of rigidity for the lightweight Chevy II chassis.

LEFT: *The biggest item on Detroit Speed's agenda for the Chevy II involved trashing the stock subframe and inner fenders. This allowed them to develop an efficient front suspension setup and use less-invasive inner fenders, allowing for additional engine bay clearance. The Mast Motorsports–prepared LS7 fits nicely in the renovated engine bay.* **RIGHT TOP:** *Oil control is a big deal in the Pro Touring world because of the extreme driving conditions. Harsh acceleration, braking, and cornering can cause problems; relieving crankcase pressure is something you should be concerned about. This tank helps relieve pressure without funky breathers on the valve covers.* **RIGHT BOTTOM:** *The cooling system for the 675-horse LS7 consists of a rather small Be Cool aluminum radiator. The Chevy II radiator support doesn't offer much room for a large radiator (20 x 24–inch maximum), but with dual electric fans, the radiator cools the all-aluminum engine with ease.*

Up front, the original subframe was tossed in the scrap pile in favor of a new Detroit Speed subframe. New frame rails and crossmembers make for a strong structure, while provisions for coil-overs, rack-and-pinion steering, and a splined anti-roll bar provide many advantages over the stock frame. Another advantage of the front subframe setup is tire and wheel clearance. The Chevy II platform has always struggled for tire clearance, and the Detroit Speed subframe provides enough room for a 9-inch-wide wheel mounted to a 255-mm-wide tire. Tubular control arms ride on top and bottom, with a set of JRi custom-tuned coil-over shocks controlling the ride. Detroit Speed spindles mount a set of Baer 6R brakes, which utilize 14-inch two-piece rotors and six-piston calipers. A matching pair of rear brakes provides even more stopping power.

Part of the advantage of the Detroit Speed front suspension system is the lack of shock towers. The inner fenders and shock towers really get in the way of any V-8 engine, so replacing the original stampings with Detroit Speed's inner fenders provides plenty of space for small-block and LS engines.

Speaking of LS engines, the Detroit Speed Chevy II test car has a killer LS7 under the hood. The naturally aspirated, 7.0-liter engine received the Mast Motorsports treatment, with a Callies crankshaft and connecting rods, as well as a set of Mahle forged pistons that create an 11.4:1 compression ratio. Highly reworked cylinder heads and a more aggressive camshaft design bring horsepower levels up to 675 at 7,250 rpm. The LS7 is controlled by a Mast M90 ECM and features an American Autowire harness to power the rest of the car's electrical system. Behind the LS7 is a Legend Gear SS-700 5-speed manual transmission, worked over by the folks at Bowler Transmission. The driveshaft is a Dynotech component that measures 3½ inches in diameter.

Externally, the car's new stance and tire and wheel combination did wonders for the car's appearance. A rather tame color combination usually doesn't make for an eye-catching car but this car makes a statement with simple and clean looks. The stock body, stock trim, and original color provide a nice contrast to the car's radical underpinnings and power plant. Although it weighs a

LEFT: *Inside, modern Recaro bucket seats feature a vintage treatment with turquoise color and stock-style inserts. The stock dash has been outfitted with an Auto Meter Stack digital dash unit, and the big original steering wheel is replaced with a Sparco racing wheel.* **MIDDLE:** *Safety harnesses are important in any form of racing but the mounting points may be the most important aspect. If these belts are mounted incorrectly, you may do more harm than good. The ideal mounting location is the horizontal bar that supports the main roll-bar hoop.* **RIGHT:** *An oversized transmission tunnel is required to fit the Legend Gear SS-700 5-speed transmission into the tight confines of the Chevy II platform. A Vintage Air heat and A/C system provides a climate-controlled cabin, while the rest of the interior is all business.*

little more than a stock Chevy II, because of the roll cage and plethora of heavy-duty suspension components, it still has plenty of pep and weighs around the 3,000-pound mark. Not bad for a Chevy II with an all-steel body, full interior, and air conditioning!

With four Recaro bucket seats, a removable Sparco steering wheel, and the protection of a roll cage and safety harnesses, the Chevy II provides race-ready details mixed with street car comforts. The original dash cluster didn't have any valuable gauges, so it was trashed in favor of an Auto Meter Stack digital dash unit, which monitors all of the engine's vital information. A Hurst shifter pokes out of the modified transmission tunnel, and the stock dash ornamentation is still in place. You won't find a radio in this lightweight car but you can enjoy the hum of a high-winding LS7 through Borla mufflers.

Just like all of Detroit Speed's test cars, the Chevy II has received its share of punishment on the autocross course, as well as on a number of long-distance road trips. It's competed in speed-stop challenges, autocross events, and drag race events, and keeps asking for more. It has run a best of 11.90 in the quarter on BFGoodrich street radials.

You could walk around this car multiple times, and even peek in the window, without realizing it has a full roll cage. The tubing is tucked very tightly against the pillars and roof skin, and it's painted to match, so the cage is nearly undetectable.

LEFT: *The compact styling of the 1963 Chevy II test car provides a fresh look and lots of performance advantages. An incredible power-to-weight ratio makes this car a handful to drive but it sticks to the racing surface and is quite the competitor.* **RIGHT:** *With mini-tubs and QUADRALink rear suspension, the Chevy II takes advantage of additional real estate for rear tires and wheels. It rolls on a set of 295/35R19 BFGoodrich tires wrapped around 19 x 10–inch wheels. Kyle retained the Nova SS trim and emblems, giving this Pro Touring beast an understated look.*

ABOVE: *On the track, the Chevy II gets plenty of abuse. Each year it is put through its paces at events such as LS Fest, where it is tasked with street driving, autocross thrashing, speed-stop challenges, and drag racing. The Chevy II handles it well, and offers a fun ride for anyone behind the wheel.* **LEFT:** *The new stance and tire and wheel combination provide a new attitude for the Chevy II test car, and it's accompanied by a completely stock body. The underpinnings are outrageous, while the exterior is clean and simple, one of Detroit Speed's specialties.*

1965 Chevelle: Simplicity Wins

Detroit Speed's fleet of test cars is immense, and it allows them to truly test new products on the street and on the racing surface. The Chevelle test car was instrumental in developing Detroit Speed's line of A-Body suspension components. The test car features the full treatment, yet still retains a lot of cool, original style. (Photo Courtesy Robert McGaffin)

If you've been around cars, especially in the racing world, you know that it isn't always the shiniest, most pristine car that takes the checkered flag or gets the most attention. Gearheads love seeing the underdog outperform a high-end car, and Detroit Speed took that approach with its 1965 Chevelle test car. Original paint and original interior make this Detroit Speed–equipped A-Body a wolf in sheep's clothing.

Kyle and Stacy Tucker concentrated heavily on the GM F-Body platform for several years, but when it was time to jump into another popular platform, the A-Body was the next in line. With applications such as 1964–1972 Chevelle, Le Mans (GTO), Cutlass (442), and Skylark (GS) under the A-Body umbrella, Detroit Speed knew the customer base would be huge. With the idea to develop a host of new products for A-Body cars, Kyle Tucker's 1965 Chevelle provided the perfect canvas for a low-key Pro Touring build.

Kyle has owned the car for more than a decade but left it in stock form for many years. Kyle and Stacy drove the car on the 2001 Hot Rod Power Tour with all stock components, including the original 327-ci small-block and Powerglide 2-speed transmission. Fast forward to 2010, and the Chevelle made its return to the Power Tour with a whole new attitude. The Pro Touring configuration proved to be much more fun to drive, even with an old-style small-block under the hood. A lowered stance, wide rubber, and a dramatically improved suspension setup turned this Chevelle from a bone-stock grocery getter into a sneaky Pro Touring machine.

As you know, the GM A-Body platform is a body-on-frame design, meaning that it features a full-perimeter frame. The A-Body also had a multi-link suspension from the factory, with coil springs on all four corners. Detroit Speed used its patented components from the F-Body world and translated them to the Chevelle test car. When all of the components were completed, the test car was outfitted with the Speed Kit 3, which is the complete package. The basic design of the front and rear suspension remain the same, but the engineering team at Detroit Speed made drastic changes to the suspension geometry to increase strength and ultimately increase traction.

Here's how they did it: The front suspension now features tubular upper and lower control arms mated to a Detroit Speed forged 2-inch drop spindle. This system is paired with a set of JRi coil-over shocks with Detroit-tuned valving, which allow Kyle to adjust the ride quality and performance quickly and easily. The Speed Kit 3 also features a splined anti-roll bar and new tie-rod ends to go with Detroit Speed's 600 steering box, which makes a huge difference in the car's responsiveness and overall feel. Big-time braking power comes from Baer 14-inch rotors and 6P six-piston calipers.

LEFT: *Yes, Detroit Speed built a car and used an old-school, carbureted small-block for power! Although most of its builds feature an LS engine, the Chevelle test car received a hand-me-down 383-ci stroker that once powered Stacy's 1969 Camaro. It's a bulletproof engine combination, and mates to a Powerglide automatic transmission. (Photo Courtesy Robert McGaffin)* **RIGHT TOP:** *Under the spun-aluminum breather is a Holley Ultra HP series carburetor rated at 650 cfm. It features billet metering blocks and a full treatment of AN fittings and braided stainless steel lines. The carburetor sits atop an Edelbrock RPM Air Gap intake manifold. (Photo Courtesy Robert McGaffin)* **RIGHT BOTTOM:** *Although the small-block Chevy is very simple by nature, it still has some trick components, including the Vintage Air Front Runner accessory drive system. The system spins a one-wire alternator, aluminum water pump, A/C compressor, and power steering pump with remote reservoir. (Photo Courtesy Robert McGaffin)*

Out back, the Chevelle features the rear Speed Kit 3, which consists of swivel-link rear control arms, coil-over shocks and springs, and an anti-roll bar. The kit also features a pair of chassis braces to help stiffen the rear section of the frame. The Chevelle test car still uses the stock GM 12-bolt rear-end housing, with the only internal upgrade consisting of a Detroit Truetrac differential. The original 3.08 gearset is still in place, as is the original Powerglide automatic transmission.

Despite the mostly original driveline, the Chevelle test car features a healthy small-block, coming in at 383 ci. The naturally aspirated small-block spent several years

LEFT: *The Chevelle test car has seen plenty of time on the autocross course but it was never thrashed hard enough to need a roll cage, racing seats, or safety harnesses. The bench seat is inviting for piling in for a lunch trip. (Photo Courtesy Robert McGaffin)* **MIDDLE:** *Looking through the spokes of the Budnik steering wheel, you see the original gauges, which leave a lot to be desired in terms of vital information. Early Chevelles didn't have real gauges, only warning lights if temperatures rise too high or if oil pressure sinks too low. (Photo Courtesy Robert McGaffin)* **RIGHT:** *With the lackluster gauge cluster in mind, Detroit Speed used the glove box for a hiding place and mounted the tachometer, water temperature, and oil pressure gauges at an angle for easy viewing. If you're going after the sleeper look, this is a great touch! (Photo Courtesy Robert McGaffin)*

LEFT TOP: *Although the Chevelle test car may have some scratches and bruises on its original paint, it's an extremely solid car and provides a great example for a low-key Pro Touring build. The low stance is provided by the Speed Kit suspension, and is complemented by a set of 18-inch Budnik wheels and BFGoodrich tires. (Photo Courtesy Robert McGaffin)* LEFT BOTTOM: *Luckily, GM A-Body cars feature deep wheel tubs from the factory, which can fit a set of 275/40R18 tires. Although nowhere near as large as some of the super-wide tires under the back of Detroit Speed's Camaro builds, the tires provide an aggressive look and ample traction. (Photo Courtesy Robert McGaffin)* RIGHT: *In motion, the Chevelle takes on a new personality: It accelerates hard, brakes hard, and corners hard. The car has excellent street manners, thanks to the mild setup, which retains the original Powerglide transmission and 3.08-geared 12-bolt rear end. (Photo Courtesy Robert McGaffin)*

under the hood of Stacy Tucker's 1969 Camaro test car, but when she decided to upgrade to an LS power plant, the 383 found a home in the Chevelle. Replacing the tired 327, the new engine is a simple setup but makes plenty of power in a budget-friendly package.

The stroked small-block is a GM Performance Parts crate engine, equipped with Vortec cast-iron cylinder heads and a Hot Cam kit, which features a hydraulic roller camshaft. It features 218 degrees of duration on the intake side and 228 degrees on the exhaust, measured at .050-inch lift. Max lift is .525 inch on both sides, and the camshaft is ground on a 112-degree lobe separation angle.

Atop the warmed-over small-block is an Edelbrock RPM Air Gap intake manifold and a Holley Ultra HP 650-cfm carburetor. An MSD Pro Billet distributor lights the fire, while off-the-shelf headers send the spent exhaust fumes into an expanse of 3-inch piping and Borla mufflers.

The test car's good looks are credited to the tire and wheel combination. It rolls on a set of Budnik Velocity wheels sized at 18 x 8 and 18 x 9 inches and wrapped in BFGoodrich rubber. With 245/40R18 and 275/40R18 tires, the Chevelle has a wide footprint, without exceeding the space of the stock wheel tubs. The gold coating on the center of the billet wheels is a nice touch that ties into the car's original Cameo Beige paint job. Adding to the car's sleeper appeal, all of the original trim and emblems are still in place, along with 50 years' worth of scratches and scrapes on the original paint.

Between the doors of Kyle's Chevelle is about as close to original as you can get. The only modification is the Budnik steering wheel, which is there because the original steering wheel was too large for Pro Touring activities. Early Chevelles had only a speedometer, clock, and fuel gauge, with "idiot lights" to indicate if the coolant temperature, oil pressure, or voltage reached a dangerous level. That explains the hidden tachometer, temperature gauge, and oil pressure gauge in the glove box. The column shifter and bench seat are still in use, and the car's only creature comfort is a Vintage Air heat and A/C unit.

The 1965 Chevelle test car put Detroit Speed's A-Body suspension components to the test on a daily basis, driving to many car shows and rod runs to compete in autocross competitions. With thousands of hard miles, the parts are still working well, and the ol' 383 is still churning out the power. The Detroit Speed Chevelle proves that a simple combination can make a very effective Pro Touring car. Although LS engines and overdrive transmissions are great, they're not mandatory if you're looking to go the Pro Touring route on a budget.

The Camaros: Eternal Test Cars

The first Detroit Speed test car is this 1969 Camaro RS/SS, owned and driven by Stacy Tucker. This photo was taken in 2008, during the car's first configuration, which tested the hydroformed subframe and QUADRALink rear suspension. The car has seen several phases, and now competes regularly in autocross events.

Kyle and Stacy Tucker entered the Pro Touring market with products for first-generation Camaros. Starting small, they developed each component until it was perfect. How did they do it? The answer is real-world testing, and Detroit Speed created a perfect way to test products, market products, and have a lot of fun. The first test car to hit the track was the famous blue 1969 Camaro, often piloted by Stacy. It has evolved in many ways but it still makes the rounds at dozens of events across the country. The second test car is Kyle's 1970 Camaro, originally built to test Detroit Speed's second-generation Camaro components. Both cars are all-out performers, and prove it every weekend during car show and racing season.

The Camaro test cars are constantly changing to increase traction and decrease weight to achieve quicker elapsed times. Here are a few details you may not notice at first glance: Stacy's test car features aluminum front fenders and a carbon-fiber hood to reduce weight; Kyle's test car has flared front fenders to fit massive 335/30R18 tires on the front.

Both test cars are LS-powered with manual transmissions, and they both have every Detroit Speed component available for purchase. Both cars feature Baer brakes, BFGoodrich tires, and Formula 43 wheels. Although they are similar in the types of products they utilize, each car has its own personality. The second-generation test car packs a bit more power, so it tends to be a little more susceptible to oversteer in the corners. This condition could also be attributed to Kyle's heavy right foot.

Overall, the test cars are used and abused on a regular basis. They're not show cars, but they put on quite a show on the autocross course. With undeniable performance on and off the track, Detroit Speed's test cars are the ultimate marketing tool for high-performance Pro Touring products. Throughout this book, you have learned that it may not be cheap, and it may not be easy, but you can make your muscle car perform better than a new Corvette without sacrificing the personality that only a muscle car possesses.

Stacy's car now features contingency decals and competes at various autocross events. The car travels the country and has a huge following, but many people may not know some of the secrets of this high-performance Camaro. For instance, the front fenders, bumper, and valance are aluminum, while the hood is carbon fiber.

Kyle and Stacy each have their own cars in competition, and it's quite common to see this husband and wife do battle on the auto-cross course. Both cars are equally potent and both drivers have tons of seat time, so it's always a close battle for bragging rights.

LEFT: This photo, from the LS Fest event in 2011, shows Kyle Tucker getting a little sideways coming out of the final corner of the autocross course. His Camaro makes big-time horsepower, and his aggressive driving style makes for some exciting moments on the track. **RIGHT:** Taken only two years later, this photo shows how the second-generation test car has evolved. It now features flared front fenders to house a pair of BFGoodrich g-Force Rival 335/30R18 tires. The car is a serious contender at any autocross event.

You can catch these two Camaro test cars on the track nearly every weekend during car show season. The Tuckers run the full Good-guys autocross schedule. They also run the Ultimate Street Car Association's schedule, which spans the United States and runs at well-known racetracks, such as Road America and Daytona International Speedway.